"This dog belongs with you. He's a special case.
He needs special handling and you're the right
person for him."

And so begins the story of Jon and the naughtiest
dog in the world . . .

THE TOTALLY TRUE STORY OF

DEVON

The Naughtiest Dog in the World

Based on the story by JON KATZ

Adapted for young readers
by Sue Cook and Ruth Knowles

RED FOX

A RED FOX BOOK 978 1 849 41110 3

First published in Great Britain by Red Fox,
an imprint of Random House Children's Books
A Random House Group Company

This edition published 2009

3 5 7 9 10 8 6 4

Text copyright © Jon Katz, 2009

Adapted for younger readers from *A Dog Year: Rescuing Devon, the most troublesome dog in the world* published in 2008 by Ebury Press, an imprint of Ebury Publishing. A Random House Group Company.
First published in the USA by Villard Books in 2002.

The right of Jon Katz to be identified as the author of this work has been asserted in accordance with the Copyright, Designs and Patents Act 1988.

The Random House Group Limited supports the Forest Stewardship Council (FSC), the leading international forest certification organization. All our titles that are printed on Greenpeace-approved FSC-certified paper carry the FSC logo. Our paper procurement policy can be found at www.rbooks. co.uk/environment.

Set in 13/20pt Bembo by Falcon Oast Graphic Art Ltd.

Red Fox Books are published by Random House Children's Books, 61–63 Uxbridge Road, London W5 5SA

www.**kids**at**randomhouse**.co.uk
www.**rbooks**.co.uk

Addresses for companies within The Random House Group Limited can be found at: www.randomhouse.co.uk/offices.htm

THE RANDOM HOUSE GROUP Limited Reg. No. 954009

A CIP catalogue record for this book is available from the British Library.

Printed and bound in Great Britain by
CPI Bookmarque, Croydon, CR0 4TD

For Paula,
who loves dogs, but not this much

CONTENTS

INTRODUCTION

This is a true story.

I love my dogs, and life with dogs is – for me – very rewarding. Dogs love purely and powerfully and without complications, and I feel so lucky to be able to share my life with them.

Devon is the Border collie star of this book and I hope you will enjoy meeting him as much as I enjoyed writing about him. This book first appeared as a longer book for adult readers, but when I travelled around with the book and my dogs (they came too, of course), we met lots of young people who wanted to know about them, and parents who asked if I could write the book again for their children to read.

This book is the result.

And my dogs (*almost* all of them) have loved children. Only Devon wasn't sure at first. But if you read his story, you will understand more about Devon – and about the challenge he brought to me in a very special dog year . . .

Jon Katz

CHAPTER ONE

One Man and His Dogs

It was morning in the Katz household and Jon, who worked as a writer, was just waking up. His dark hair rested on the pillow, and his glasses on the bedside table twinkled in the early morning sunlight.

Downstairs, Julius and Stanley, the family's two dogs, snoozed happily too. Their ears twitched, their paws shifted position now and then – and sometimes they let out a rumble of doggy snores.

Julius and Stanley were Labradors – big dogs

with silky golden coats the colour of butter, floppy ears and long wagging tails. They had lived with Jon and his wife, Paula, for a long time now and they all loved each other more than anything.

Jon had brought Julius home when he was just a puppy. "I've got a surprise for you!" he'd told Emma, his daughter, holding the wriggling doggy bundle out to the little girl, smiling at the puzzled frown on her face.

Emma had looked amazed as she'd moved her head close to Julius's.

Looking up at the shrieking girl, Julius had blinked, stuck out his long tongue and licked her nose. Jon had patted the puppy's head, and Julius had licked him too. They looked at each other for a moment, and somehow both of them had known at once that they would be friends.

A year later, his cousin Stanley had arrived. He came from the same breeder as Julius, and looked almost identical to the older dog when *he*'d moved in.

This tiny new puppy had melted Jon's heart straight away, though he had wondered whether

Julius would take to the newcomer. However, Stanley had soon won him over, and within a couple of days the two dogs loved each other and their new family as much as Jon and his family loved them.

It was now seven years since Stanley had joined the family. He and Julius were much bigger – and still the best of friends. Julius was eight years old and Stanley seven, but sometimes they behaved as if they were much older! They were both lazy dogs: all they wanted to do most of the time was rest! Sometimes Stanley would summon up the energy to chase a ball or have a swim in a pond, but apart from that the Labradors" days proceeded at a nice, comfortable, relaxed pace and they were happy with their quiet life!

Jon came downstairs for a glass of water and looked in on the dogs, waking them. As he went back upstairs, they followed him for their morning cuddle. Jon smiled, as he did every time he looked at his calm and loving pets, thinking for the millionth time how lucky he was to have them.

Dog Report

Name:	Julius
Age:	Eight
Breed:	Golden Labrador
Lives:	With Jon and Paula, in New York
Friends:	Everybody! But especially Jon and Stanley
Likes:	Sleeping, lots of hugs, rawhide chews, dinner, walks, sniffing interesting smells, staring at the tops of mountains for hours
Doesn't like:	Rainy days, (he's allergic to rainy days), the sea (he's allergic to sea water)

Dog Report

Name: Stanley

Age: Seven

Breed: Golden Labrador

Lives: With Jon and Paula, in New York

Friends: Everybody! But especially Jon and Julius

Likes: Sleeping, lots of hugs, biscuits, dinner, chasing balls, sniffing interesting smells, swimming in ponds, playing tug-of-war with rope toys

Doesn't like: Rainy days

A typical day for Jon, Julius and Stanley:

Getting up

Neither dog moves a muscle until Jon is awake, then they slither into his bed for a big furry family cuddle. Wet noses and the odd lick are normal! After Jon is up, they sit quietly and attentively under the kitchen table, staring at their food bowls. *If we stare hard enough and long enough, will our food magically appear?* they wonder!

Early walk

This is a leisurely stroll of about half an hour through the local neighbourhood. Julius and Stanley want to sniff *everything*. No shrub or rock is missed and nothing can distract them when they smell something particularly interesting. The walks are peaceful, and they meet lots of dog buddies, friends and admirers. Everyone likes Julius and Stanley and the local children wave at them from bikes and car windows.

Note: Labradors are supposed to be hunting dogs – outdoor working dogs – but Julius and Stanley have never been keen on rain or snow. If the weather is nasty, they have mastered a hundred-metre dash to the nearest tree, and then they want to go back inside. This suits Jon nicely – he's not keen on walking in the rain either!

Snack time

This is two big rawhide chews with a layer of peanut butter in between. Jules and Stanley carry these treats into the garden and settle down for a good gnaw. This kind of thing can be pretty tiring for a dog and they need a good long rest afterwards, sometimes rousing themselves from their nap to bark at a passing dog. Mostly not.

Daytime

Jon works from home as a writer, which means he gets to spend *lots* of time with Stanley and Julius. It's a good thing they all get along so well! He works in his study; if it's rainy, the two dogs come in and act as footrests, both tucked underneath his desk, one on the left, one on the right; otherwise they nap in the sun. The dogs are clever, knowing exactly when Jon has an important deadline and needs to be left in peace.

Afternoon walk

This is maybe a mile or so, but no one's in any hurry – it's a gentle stroll.

More snacks

Jon knows that he shouldn't give his boys snacks, but he can't resist offering them rawhide chews, pigs' ears and dog biscuits . . .

Dinner

Julius and Stanley like this time of day! But it doesn't take them long to scoff down their food.

Bedtime

As night falls, so the Labs settle down on their

beds for a final snack and then fall into a deep, unmoving sleep.

Later, out on their morning walk, Julius and Stanley padded along the familiar pavements, totally contented. After a while Stanley nipped Jon's bottom to get his attention. He wanted Jon to throw his ball for him to go and catch.

He didn't need to do anything else: Jon knew exactly what he wanted and threw the ball into the grass ahead. Stanley yapped happily and raced after it.

We could all do this in our sleep, Jon thought as they strolled along. They were almost like a school of fish, the three of them, veering first in one direction, then another. They turned corners at the same time, knew each other's moods and were happy sitting in silence together in various parks and gardens, sharing their lunch.

The three of them enjoyed their walk in the sun, little knowing that things were about to change for ever. And the change was coming on four legs . . .

CHAPTER TWO

The Arrival of Devon

A few days later, Jon got a phone call. He'd barely had time to say hello before the woman on the other end of the phone introduced herself as Deanne, a Border collie breeder. She had read one of Jon's books in which he'd mentioned how much he loved dogs, and had looked him up. Now she started talking very quickly and very loudly, and it took Jon a few moments to catch up with what she was saying . . .

"This dog *belongs* with you," Deanne told him.

"He's a special case. He needs special handling and I really think you're the right person for him . . ." She went on to tell him all about Devon, a Border collie she had bred. The dog had been trained by his owner to compete in obedience competitions, but he had stopped performing as well as he used to and wasn't winning anything any more. Devon's owners no longer wanted him and had given him back to Deanne. The poor little collie was feeling rejected and unloved – and he needed a good home.

Jon shook his head, even though Deanne, on the other end of the phone, couldn't see him. He was happy with his life here, he thought. He didn't think Paula would want any more dogs, Emma didn't live at home anymore and *he* was happy with things the way they were too. He was just about to say no . . .

"Please, Jon," Deanne begged. "I just know you can give him the right home. He really needs someone who won't mind a bit of odd behaviour."

Jon looked through the window at Julius and

Stanley, who were napping in the sun. He thought of their peaceful, contented threesome. He already had two happy dogs who didn't demonstrate any "odd behaviour", and he had a very busy life. He knew what he *should* be saying, but he couldn't bring himself to actually utter the words. "OK," he told Deanne reluctantly. "I'll talk to Paula and Emma about it . . ."

Jon could hear the smile in her voice at his words! What had he done? he wondered. He didn't know very much about Border collies: he realized he'd better do some research . . .

What Jon *did* know about Border collies already was this:

- They were medium-sized dogs that looked a bit like small shaggy black-and-white wolves.
- They were very intelligent.
- They needed lots of space – vast areas to roam. Mountains and moors were ideal. He knew you didn't see a lot of mountains and

moorlands in a suburb outside a big city like his – you didn't see many Border collies, either.

- They had heaps of energy; they'd go crazy living shut up in a house all day while a family went out to work.

- They were developed as dogs to herd sheep.

- They loved to chase things – squirrels, rabbits, cars: anything that moved away from them. And they could run at blinding speeds.

Deanne called often over the next few days. This was a big decision for Jon and his family, and for Deanne, so they all needed to get as much information as they could to make sure the little Border collie found the right home. What Jon knew so far concerned *normal* Border collies. But the more information Deanne gave him, the more he realized that Devon was not a normal Border collie . . .

What Jon learned about Devon was this:

- He was two years old.
- He was very, very bright.
- He was well-bred but really highly strung.
- He had never lived in a house before, or with just one human.
- He was in big trouble and needed a new home – badly . . .

Jon ran this list of facts about Devon over and over in his mind. *Stop! Danger ahead!* he kept telling himself. But he just couldn't bring himself to say no to this dog in need. He sat at his desk and put his head in his hands. What should he do? This dog needed him.

He looked down at Julius and Stanley, who were lying under his feet. They were both well-behaved and loving, gentle with children and good-humoured. "Look at them," Jon said to himself. "I trained Julius and Stanley, so maybe I *can* take on Devon too. If I'm good with dogs, then

I should use my skills and give this needy young animal a loving home, shouldn't I?" *That's it!* he decided suddenly. "Boys," he told the Labradors triumphantly, "we're going to do it! We're going to give Devon a home."

Once his decision had been made, the time seemed to fly by. There was lots to do to prepare for the newest member of Jon's family, and in what seemed like no time at all he was heading for the airport to meet Devon. The lonely little Border collie was being flown east from Texas to start his new life with Jon just outside New York.

Jon was excited – he couldn't wait to meet Devon, but he couldn't lie: he was nervous too, and he did have a lot of worries. He still didn't know very much about the dog, apart from the fact that he needed a new home badly; he didn't even know what he looked like! Would he be up to the challenge? And what would Julius and Stanley think of the newcomer?

"Boys," Jon announced solemnly before he

left for the airport, "today's the day. I'm bringing another dog here – Devon. He might be a little wacky. Be patient."

Julius and Stanley looked at him fondly, their tails wagging. They could tell that their master was stressed about something, and they rubbed themselves patiently up against his legs in an attempt to calm him down. But neither they nor Jon had any idea how much trouble was heading towards them!

The airport was very busy and Devon's flight had been delayed. *Poor Devon*, Jon thought to himself as he paced up and down the arrivals hall. *The poor little guy's already been holed up in the plane near the noisy engines with everybody's heavy luggage – delays are the last thing he needs.* When he finally did get out of his crate, he'd probably be terrified. It was bedlam at the airport – luggage everywhere, people shouting, loudspeakers blaring, and crowds of passengers coming and going. Jon felt nervous himself as he stood there waiting for Devon – and he was *used* to airports. How would poor Devon feel?

Finally, after Jon had paced around the arrivals area for about an hour, he saw Devon's plane land outside on the runway. He caught the attention of a member of staff. "Is there a dog on that plane?" he asked. When the woman nodded, he smiled. In a matter of minutes Devon would be part of his family!

He stared fixedly at the arrivals gate in case he missed seeing Devon taking his first steps in New York. Finally, at 9p.m., two baggage handlers pulled a large blue dog-travelling crate noisily across the airport floor. Devon's crate was enormous! It had air holes along the sides and a metal grille over the front opening. On top rested an envelope with the dog's travel papers inside. Jon stepped forward excitedly. He had planned to reach into the crate, put on Devon's new blue collar and lead, and take him out to the car park as quickly as possible, away from the madness inside the airport. But as he looked into the crate, Jon realized that his plan was not going to come off as smoothly as he had thought!

There was a blanket scrunched up against the door of the cage and lots of shredded newspaper on the bottom. Jon took all this in carefully – but he couldn't actually see Devon himself! All he could make out was flashes of black and white circling round and round and round inside the crate. Devon was obviously desperate to get out!

"Devon," Jon called softly. "Devon, I'm going to open the door, boy. It's going to be OK." He had always talked to Julius and Stanley, and his Labradors seemed to understand him perfectly, but Devon clearly did not! As soon as Jon knelt to undo the latch, a blur of black and white fur shot past him into the crowd. The gate slammed open into Jon's face. "*Oof!*" he exclaimed as the force knocked him flat on his back.

Devon was out of sight before Jon could even scramble to his feet. When he did stand up again, he could see no sign of the dog, and only the shrieks and shouts from the crowds around the airport told Jon which way he was headed.

Devon was confused and frightened. He raced from one baggage carousel to another, then back again, desperately looking for a way out. Two baggage handlers and three policemen joined Jon in chasing after Devon, but whenever any of them got close to him, he turned and dashed in the other direction, vanishing into the crowds again.

Devon wheeled round,

and kept running

and running

and running.

Faster and faster.

He was out of control.

And he was also very frightened.

Jon was frightened too. The men trying to help him catch the little dog were getting impatient. "I think we need to call in the animal-control team," one of them grunted. "This crazy animal could bite a child or knock someone over – then there'll be trouble."

"I've seen dogs a lot less excited than this one bite people," another officer agreed.

Jon knew the men were right. A panicky dog in a strange place could be *very* dangerous. But he didn't know what to do. What if Devon dashed out of the doors and got loose in the car park or on the roads? He could be hit by a car . . .

Jon tried to stay calm. "Devon! Devon!" he called. There was no response. Devon wasn't slowing down for anyone.

Half an hour later, just as Jon was starting to wonder whether he *should* let the policemen call in the animal-control team, they finally managed to corner Devon. Jon knelt down in front of his new dog and took his first proper look at him.

Devon was beautiful, and Jon smiled down at him, despite the chaos he had just caused. The collie was sleek and black, with a pointed nose, a narrow white blaze on his forehead and a white chest. He was very skinny, and Jon could see that he had not enjoyed being cooped up in the travelling cage for hours. His fur was matted with sweat, and his body was hunched. He was panting heavily and his lovely dark eyes looked very, very sad. Jon knew at that moment that he had done the right thing – more than anything he needed to help this animal.

"Devon," he said softly, reaching out with one hand towards the scared dog. "Stay, Devon. Stay."

Jon had done a lot of reading about dogs like Devon over the past weeks, and all the books had said how important it was to make eye contact. In the wild, eye contact was how Border collies controlled sheep, and Jon knew that if he could catch Devon's eye now, the dog might obey him. Still speaking gently, he continued, "I'm your new friend. It's OK now. Stay, boy. I'm going to take you home." He repeated the words soothingly over and over again to try and calm the frightened young Border collie.

Jon slowly pulled a dog biscuit from his trouser pocket. He placed it on the ground and nudged it towards Devon.

The dog ignored the biscuit. The look in his sad eyes made Jon feel bad; it was as if he was saying, *Do you think I can be bribed that easily?* His eyes darted everywhere, carefully taking in everybody

– including Jon. Jon wondered if he was looking for another escape route, but for now the dog stayed where he was.

He decided to take his chance while Devon was calmer. "Stay," he said again. "Stay, Devon. It's OK." Devon raised his head and looked at the man carefully. Jon leaned forward and the collie allowed him to scratch him gently behind the ear.

Suddenly someone gave a loud shout nearby and Devon jerked away from Jon, scared by the noise. He tossed his head around, his eyes frightened.

Jon was worried that Devon might run off again, but he persisted: he needed to make friends with this dog. He carried on stroking his soft fur and then patted him on the shoulder. Very slowly and carefully he slipped on Devon's new collar and lead.

Devon stared up at Jon, looking him right in the eye. He looked as if he understood that this was his new master, and that they were going home together.

CHAPTER THREE

And Devon Makes . . . Three!

"Heel!" Jon finally walked out of the airport with Devon on his new lead, exhausted and relieved. The Border collie was no longer trying to escape, and he trotted calmly through the car park alongside Jon. Now that he was under control, Devon paid attention to everything around him. He stared at all the traffic and people, turning his head when he noticed, heard or smelled something new and interesting.

When they reached Jon's van, Jon pulled out a jug of water and poured it into a bowl, letting Devon slurp it up greedily — it had been hours since he'd had anything to eat or drink and he was thirsty. Jon knelt on the pavement next to the dog and offered him another biscuit. This time Devon gobbled it up quickly, followed by another, and then another!

Jon leaned forward and scratched his head. Devon's ears came up — he was starting to relax. Jon smiled. This was a good sign. A dog's ears are a great way of seeing what they're thinking. When the ears come up, a dog is usually paying attention to something; Jon hoped that meant Devon was paying attention to him!

But the very next moment a huge noisy jet flew overhead and the terrified dog cringed away from the din. He gazed about in a panic, first at Jon, then up at the sky and then back again.

Jon looked down into Devon's eyes as he stroked his soft head. They were astonishingly expressive. "Devon, listen to me, pal. It's going to be OK," he told him.

And Devon seemed to listen. When the next plane flew over, he didn't seem quite as scared, and by the time the third and fourth jets took off, he didn't even flinch.

He and Jon stared at each other in silence for a while before Jon spoke again. "We're going to go home," he told Devon. "I'll stay with you; I'll give you lots of walks, lots of food and lots of patience. I'll take good care of you. Let's try it, OK?"

Devon looked as if he was thinking carefully about what Jon had just said. Jon held out his hand, and Devon moved forward and licked it. *Deal!* he seemed to be saying. *Let's be friends.*

Fifteen minutes later, they were home. Stanley and Julius lumbered over to the fence, tails wagging, ready to say hello, as they always did whenever Jon came home. They padded over to the driveway to see what was going on: Jon had a strange dog with him and they didn't know who he was!

Jon looked on anxiously, hoping his Labradors would be patient with this new member of the family. Two dogs were a pair, but three dogs made a pack. In a pack there were often fights over food and love. Would his new pack get along together?

Dog Report: First impressions

Name:	*Devon*
Age:	*Two*
Breed:	*Border collie*
Home:	*Raised in Texas, living in fenced-in fields with scores of other dogs day and night*
Personality:	*Scared and upset! He doesn't trust people and just wants to run away*
Jon's challenge:	*To love this difficult dog, and win his love and trust in return*

Jon thought Julius would be OK – he had an accepting nature – but Stanley might be more hostile and Jon didn't think he'd want to lose his spot as number two in the pack. The three dogs cautiously touched noses with each other, saying a brief hello.

Jon knew that how he handled this introduction of Devon to Stanley and Julius and his new house was very important – things could get tricky. He decided to take Devon for a short walk; it might calm him down again and get him used to the area. Turning away from the Labradors, Jon kept Devon on his leash and headed down the road. Beside him, his new dog had his nose to the ground, sniffing the pavement. He seemed much calmer now that he was out in the fresh air, and for a moment Jon felt himself relax. This wasn't going to be as bad as he had thought at the airport, he told himself.

Mistake!

With a sharp jerk of the lead, tearing it out of Jon's hand, Devon was gone!

"Devon! Stop! Where are you?" he yelled.

Spinning round in all directions, he could see no trace of the collie. He panicked. There was no animal-control team to help him now.

Suddenly he spotted a passing van driving along the road – with Devon perched up high on the roof. He zoomed past, looking cheekily back at his new master! At first Jon could not believe his eyes. He stood there in amazement – dogs couldn't *fly*, yet Devon was so high up, and moving so quickly, that's exactly what it looked like he was doing.

Pooper-scooper in hand, Jon gave chase! "Hey! Hey, stop! Stop, there's a dog on the car!" he yelled in a panic, trying to get the van driver's attention.

The van slowed – the driver looking back at Jon, mystified – and as he did so, Devon nimbly hopped off and headed back towards Jon, as if he'd done nothing wrong.

"Sit!" Jon screamed. He was cross now, and Devon realized this and obeyed him instantly. He looked up at his new owner in bewilderment. *Why are you making such a noise?* he seemed to be asking. *What have I done wrong? That was* fun!

★ ★ ★

Left behind in the garden, Jon's Labradors were puzzled too. They knew that something important was happening but they weren't sure what. Their tails wagged as they waited patiently for their master to return with his strange new friend.

They could smell him coming closer and looked up from where they lay. The fur along Stanley's back stood up and he gave a low growl at the back of his throat.

Julius was calmer, but he decided to totally ignore the young newcomer for now. He padded over to Jon, licking him hello again as if Devon wasn't there at all.

Devon waited quietly by Jon's side. Jon held his breath. After a minute Stanley joined the group too. The dogs stared at each other in silence. They circled and sniffed each other again and again, but to Jon's relief there was no snarling or fighting. He decided it was fine to let Devon into the house now.

Jon opened the back door and the Labs lumbered

up into the house that was so familiar to them. As the new dog, Devon should've followed them, but he . . .

. . . leaped right over the top of Stanley, taking the steps into the house in two hops. He raced into the living room,

pivoted sharply,

dashed into the kitchen,

jumped onto the kitchen table,

then jumped off again.

Jon thought Devon had gone mad. Julius and Stanley looked as if they agreed; they all stood and stared at him. It was like watching a speeded-up film as the Border collie whizzed back and forth about the house like some kind of unstoppable machine.

The frantic behaviour didn't seem to be getting any better. Devon lapped up some water, then raced from room to room, running back every now and then to check where Jon was. Soon, the dog had a circuit going –

to the back door,

to the front door,

to his food bowl,

then his water bowl,

back to the living room,

then round again to the back door.

Jon, Julius and Stanley continued to stare at each other in astonishment. What had they brought into their house? This dog had serious amounts of energy!

Devon was even more frantic and unsettled than Jon had expected, and as the dog raced around the house, his master wondered again if he could actually look after him. Deanne had told Jon that after he'd been brought back, Devon had felt unloved. "The best thing you can do," she'd told Jon, "is to persuade him that you love him and that you'll stick with him no matter what."

Staring at the Border collie now, Jon remembered Deanne's words. Of course he could do this – he'd show Devon that somebody loved him and would stick with him through thick and thin.

CHAPTER FOUR

Trouble!

It was a strange first night together for Jon and Devon. Although he did eventually stop charging about the house, the dog still wanted to keep his new master in sight at all times. When Julius and Stanley settled themselves down for the night in their cosy dog beds, Devon padded after Jon up the stairs and into his bedroom, waiting to be told what to do next. Jon told him to sit, and the dog obediently dropped to the floor at the side of the bed. His eyes didn't leave Jon all night . . .

The next morning Jon realized he was going to have trouble walking all three dogs at the same time. After Devon's flying van performance, he knew it would be dangerous to let him walk off-lead, so, after unlocking the back door to allow all three dogs into the back garden, he decided to walk the Labradors first. He let them out of the garden and carefully shut the gate behind him, leaving Devon where he was.

Jon, Julius and Stanley started out along their familiar route. But they had not been going for more than a minute when Jon sensed something behind him. He turned, and gasped in shock. There, sitting on the pavement, was Devon, staring up at him. Jon looked back towards his house and saw that the gate was still locked. The fence was too high for Devon to have jumped it, so Jon had no idea how on earth the dog had made it out here.

Still in shock, he reached out to grab Devon's collar and take him back to the garden, but the collie clearly did not like this idea. He'd been outraged to find himself left behind while Jon went off in the sunshine with Julius and Stanley, and he wasn't going back! He dashed away across the street without even looking out for any traffic and hurtled towards the school on the next corner.

Jon was gobsmacked. Shooing Julius and Stanley quickly back into the garden, he raced after Devon. He tore down the street, finally reaching the school completely out of breath and covered in sweat. He jumped as he heard the ominous sounds of shouting and blaring horns, and turned to see a big yellow school bus outside the school. He was not too surprised to see Devon crouched in a herding position in front of the vehicle, barking furiously and nipping at the tyres.

Border collies are working dogs. On farms all round the world, they herd flocks of sheep, racing around fields and driving the flock to exactly where the shepherd wants them. It's their natural instinct. There weren't any sheep in New York that Jon knew of. But as Devon had just discovered, there *were* buses – and now he wanted to herd one of those.

"No, no!" Jon yelled, not even stopping to wonder how ridiculous he sounded. "It's not a sheep. It's not a sheep!" Nobody paid any attention – especially not Devon.

The bus driver was getting more and more angry. He couldn't move unless Devon got out of the way, and he was losing his temper. His face went red and he shouted at the dog, keeping his hand on the bus horn. Some parents yelled too, but Devon just ignored the noise, focusing all his attention on the tyres in front of him, determined not to let the big yellow bus move one single centimetre without his say-so.

"Stay!" Jon raced to Devon's side and gave him a little smack on the bottom to get his attention. It didn't have quite the effect he wanted: Devon was delighted! He thought that Jon was finally here to join in with his herding, and his ears pricked up with happiness. This was the best thing that had happened to him since he'd left Texas!

The collie's big dark eyes stared at Jon. It took him a little while to work out that Jon was not as happy as he was, and then he hung his head guiltily.

Jon needed to get Devon out of there. Having got his attention, he dragged him away by his collar. All the parents scowled as he passed them – Jon didn't know where to look. He tried to apologize. "He's a sheepdog," he called out. "He's like Babe, you know?"

Once he was away from all the frowning faces, Jon yanked Devon over to a bench and sat down crossly. "You can't do that, Devon," he told him. "You can't run off like that. You can't run away."

Jon's heart pounded. He knew that Devon could so easily have been killed as he raced across the streets. He could also have got into a lot of trouble as he tried to herd the bus. *All this after only a day together*, he thought. He felt terrible too. He had actually smacked Devon to get his attention. It had only been a little tap, Jon knew, but he wished he hadn't needed to do it. He had just been so scared for Devon, so desperate to get him to safety.

Lost in his thoughts, Jon didn't notice Devon

climbing up onto the bench. He crept onto his new master's lap, then leaned up to lick his face. Jon hugged him tightly and Devon wagged his tail for the first time since arriving at his new home.

CHAPTER FIVE

The Battle of the Gate

The next day Jon decided he couldn't risk leaving Devon in the garden again while he walked Julius and Stanley. He still had no idea how the naughty little dog had made it out onto the pavement – he might get up to all sorts of trouble if he escaped a second time. "You're going to have to stay indoors today, Devon," he told the dog with a sigh.

Devon did not look impressed.

When Jon came back into the house after his

walk, he gasped in shock. His telephone and answering machine lay in pieces on the floor. "Oh, Devon!" he sighed as he tried to pick up the bits and put them back together again.

It was as if Devon was showing Jon exactly how he felt about being locked inside. He had taken his temper out on the phone!

But Jon could not be cross for very long because Devon was so delighted to see him again. He raced around the room, barking loudly, tail wagging, before rushing over to say hello. "Down, Devon, down . . ." Jon tried. But the Border collie hurled himself excitedly at him – happy, happy, happy!

As soon as he'd said hello, Devon was desperate to get outside again. Being cooped up indoors all day was boring and he raced happily into the garden.

Jon knew that he had been right the first time – Devon was much happier outdoors and he obviously *hated* being shut in the house. Jon didn't want to think about which treasured belongings might be broken the next day if he made Devon stay indoors again! *Maybe he'll stay in the garden when I leave tomorrow*, he thought. He was wrong!

"Stay, Devon. Just stay in the garden and I'll be back very soon," Jon told the Border collie firmly the next morning. There was a tall white picket fence all round the garden that he thought should have kept Devon in – it had always contained Julius and Stanley – but it obviously hadn't last time so Jon knew he had to be careful.

He double-checked that the garden gate was locked, then drove off, leaving Devon behind. He had only gone a few metres when he looked back. There was Devon, sitting on the pavement *outside* the garden – again!

Jon tried again the next day.

And again.

Each time he came back to find Devon sitting on the pavement outside the garden. Jon simply could not work out how Devon was doing it. How was he getting out? And more importantly, how could he keep him in?

Jon decided to see if he could catch Devon in the act! He left the little dog in the garden, and got into his car as if he was leaving. Then, instead of setting off down the road, he quickly drove round to the front door, before jumping out of the car, running through the house to the window, to see if he could catch Devon escaping. But it was no good. It looked as though Devon was behaving himself today. He was sitting in the garden exactly where Jon had left him, his tail wagging, staring at his master through the window.

Devon didn't understand what was going on. He thought Jon had gone off in his car, but to his delight his master was back already and wanted to say hello! He barked excitedly.

Jon tried to catch Devon another way. This time he actually drove off, but parked a few roads away. He sneaked back on foot and quietly tiptoed through to the rear of the house again. Going down onto his hands and knees, he crawled up to the window and peeped through. *Aha!* Everything suddenly fell into place. He could see exactly how Devon had been making his escape – and he could not believe how clever this dog was!

Jon watched as Devon showed him what he had been doing. He raced up and down the garden to check each of the slats in the fence, then he snuffled his long nose into the spaces between them. When he found a loose one, he wiggled his nose furiously, pushing the wood to one side, and managed to squeeze himself through the narrow opening he had made.

Jon was absolutely amazed. When he had got through the space, Devon was even smart enough to turn round and push the slat *back into position* from the other side of the fence so nobody would be able to see how he had got out. No wonder he had been able to keep escaping from the garden: he had been hiding the evidence, leaving no trace of his route.

Jon rushed out to confront Devon, but the dog just stared defiantly back at him. *If you leave me alone, you'll pay for it*, is what he seemed to be saying. As with the broken telephone, it was as if Jon was being punished for daring to keep Devon cooped up.

Devon had such a mixture of personality traits. He was sometimes nervous and scared, but also full of energy – and as Jon had just seen, very, very stubborn. Though he was impressed with Devon's clever escape plan, Jon was angry. It wasn't safe to have a dog loose on the streets. Devon could be killed, or he could cause an accident . . . And now Jon knew how easily this could happen. He realized that shouting at Devon wouldn't work. Unless he could catch him in the very act of doing wrong – at the exact moment it happened – it would do no good: Devon would only be confused, and wonder why Jon didn't love him any more. How was he going to train this naughty little dog?

Jon decided to leave it for now, but he also decided to play Devon at his own game. He nailed the loose fence slat shut!

Over the next few days Devon found another loose slat – which Jon nailed shut too. Then another. Then half a dozen more.

Devon sat watching as Jon hammered every single slat into place.

"You are *not* getting out of this garden!" Jon told him sternly.

Devon cocked his head as if he was listening carefully. But he wasn't happy. He hated being left all by himself.

And later that day, when Jon took Julius and Stanley out again without Devon, he came back to find his new dog sitting on the grass at the front of the house and the porch door swinging open. Devon had learned to open the door with his paw!

CHAPTER SIX

Beginning to Bond?

Julius and Stanley had been trained to walk off-lead since they were puppies and neither of them had any interest nowadays in chasing anything but a sunny spot in the garden, let alone a bus. They would never have found the energy to explore like Devon wanted to!

Jon often grinned to himself when he considered the differences between his pets. If he were to draw a map of a typical walk with Julius and Stanley, it would show two long straight lines that stuck mostly to the pavement. Jon would amble along with his hands in his pockets, lost in his thoughts, not needing to worry about the Labradors at all. Julius would sometimes veer off a bit to sniff a bush – he liked to take his time when they walked; or Stanley might dash after his blue ball when Jon threw it for him – but basically they liked to stay on the pavement and follow their usual route – the route they took every day.

Devon was very different! He *always* wanted to chase things. He never stopped rushing to and fro, panting. Jon had no idea if he'd be able to draw a sketch of *his* walks. It would show all sorts of crazy circles, with arrows shooting out in every direction. Devon –

trotted a couple of metres ahead,

then circled Jon a few times,

headed off the other way,

went to investigate every single driveway and footpath they passed,

loped around every single bush as if he thought there might be a stray sheep hiding behind it, then darted ahead again . . .

Jon seemed to be continually shouting, "Come *here*, Devon!"

But after a few long, exhausting walks like this Jon realized exactly what his new dog was doing. When he watched carefully, he saw that Devon was trying to *herd* him, just like he had done with the bus! Wherever they walked, Devon always kept him in sight and behaved exactly like a Border collie would if Jon was a sheep: he never strayed too far from him and came back constantly to check where he was!

Jon wanted to be proper friends with Devon: the dog had to recognize him as his master and stop treating him like a sheep! One of the books he had on Border collies suggested brushing. Apparently collies loved being brushed down; it could really help a dog and his owner to bond. So one morning, with the Labs happily occupied in the garden, chewing on their peanut-butter snacks, Jon decided to go for it. He put a special metal-toothed dog brush in his pocket and picked up Devon's lead. "Come on, boy," he said. "Let's go to the park."

Devon clearly didn't need a second invitation. A walk? Great! He barked excitedly.

When they reached the park, Jon found a secluded bench – a place where there were no dogs, people or cars to distract them. Pulling out the brush, he began to groom Devon gently, using long strokes down his back, haunches and chest.

For the first time since his arrival, Devon seemed almost relaxed. His tail swished slowly back and forth and Jon saw that beneath all the crazy energy, Devon was a big softie. He clearly loved the attention. Jon was pleased: the brushing had definitely calmed the Border collie down – even if it wasn't for very long! – so Jon decided to brush him like this every day.

A couple of days later, Jon put down his brush once the grooming session was over. Devon stared up at him with his big dark eyes, then reached up and put his paws on Jon's shoulders, as if he was hugging him! Jon was ecstatic, and he hugged him straight back. "It's OK, boy," he told him again and again. "It's OK now." He hoped that Devon was finally starting to trust him.

Soon, brushing was an important part of Devon's daily routine, and eventually Jon only had to say, "Come on, Devon, let's go get brushed!" and the collie would glance at the brush, then dart over to the back door, knowing exactly where they were going and what was happening.

On their journeys to the park, Jon also began to notice that Devon didn't circle or chase or herd him any more. He padded calmly beside his master, looking pleased with himself, and Jon wondered if Devon was beginning to accept that he would take care of him. He knew he needed to work hard at winning Devon over and making him feel loved, and slowly but surely it seemed to be working – thanks to the brushing. He wondered if giving Devon positive attention in other ways would help too.

Jon began to praise Devon for everything he did

that wasn't naughty. If the young dog walked a few metres in a straight line, or if he finished his own dinner and left the Labs' bowls alone, Jon praised him. If he came when he was called, he was praised too. "Good boy, Devon. Good, good boy." Jon said it over and over again – two hundred times a day sometimes – and Devon loved it!

Soon the collie started to believe Jon; his ears were pricked, his chest stood out, and his paintbrush tail was held high and proud. He looked magnificent! His black and white coat was glossy after all the brushing and he had a mischievous glint in his eyes. People began to stop and admire him; he was almost unrecognizable from the frightened dog who had stepped off the plane from Texas. He had never had attention, love or companionship in his life before; now he had all three, and he was clearly enjoying it.

But for Devon and Jon there was still a lot to learn . . .

★ ★ ★

You might like these wonderful photographs of Jon's dogs.

Enjoy looking through them!

PROGRESS REPORT

THINGS TO WORK ON WITH DEVON

Walking off the lead: *Needs improvement*

Coming when called: *Needs improvement – will only come when he wants to*

Staying in the garden: *This is a big problem. He can get out of the garden any time he wants to, in a variety of ways. My neighbour told me that once he saw Devon simply leap over the fence. When he got bored with trying all the slats, he tunnelled under the fence instead*

Bad habits indoors: *Opening doors and cupboards, piling up shoes, taking loaves of bread upstairs and putting them on* the bed . . . He doesn't deliberately damage anything, but lots of stuff is getting broken. He's telling me that every time I leave him, he's going to cause trouble

Bad habits outdoors: Digging craters - he can dig a bomb-sized hole in minutes, as he does when he's tunnelling under the fence

Bad habits when out on a walk: Chasing cars and lorries - if something passes us on our walks, he'll dash after it, pulling me so hard that he nearly rips the lead out of my hands or pulls me over. He particularly likes chasing big, loud things

"Devon," Jon said as he hugged the collie after they had been together for some weeks, "are you the naughtiest dog in the world?" He stared into those clever, deep brown eyes, and Devon licked him on the chin a few times before squirming to get down. He was a very *wriggly* dog, and hated being still for more than a few minutes at a time.

Jon was slowly getting used to Devon and all his character traits and habits. He knew that some breeds of dog were very calm and placid. Others were bred to retrieve things – on the land or from water; others to dig holes or to use their noses to follow a scent. Some dogs only needed short walks each day; others liked to be on the go all the time, working. Jon knew that Border collies belonged to this last group. They needed to keep busy, to see things and go places, to chew stuff, run around, dig holes and be part of everything that was happening. They were very clever animals, so if there was nothing about that really interested them, they would find something else to do.

Jon was discovering that, in Devon's case, this tended to be something *naughty*. Daily life became a battle between the two of them, and Devon was determined to get his way. Sometimes the dog just made Jon feel so frustrated, and from time to time he lost his temper completely. When this happened, Stanley and Julius would look on, cocking their heads to one side, puzzled. They didn't like it when Jon yelled, even if it wasn't at them, and they would drop to the ground with their ears pinned back nervously in case their master began to shout in their direction too.

When Jon first got the Labradors, he'd had dog-training sessions with a professional, to teach *him* how to teach *them* to come when called, to sit, stay, lie down and walk beside him without a lead – all the things Julius and Stanley now did almost without thinking. Jon knew that he now needed to put what he had learned with them into effect with Devon.

The two most important things were:

- To make sure Devon understood Jon. He knew they could be great pals – and Devon already knew that Jon would spoil him rotten and was good at hugs.

- To make sure that Devon also knew that Jon was the boss, that Jon was the leader of this pack – not Devon. All dogs are pack animals and they need to understand exactly where they rank in the pack. The dog should never be number one or there would be problems.

Listing it like this made the training sound easy, but Devon was now already two years old – that was a *teenager* in dog terms – and he hadn't had the training most puppies get when they are very young. The challenge for Jon now that he and Devon were familiar with each other was to figure out how he could train the collie while building up his confidence at the same time. Whatever had happened to him at his first home had obviously left him feeling as if he wasn't much good at being a dog, so he needed to feel better about himself too before he could really be happy.

The one big problem was that Devon would still not do what he was told. Jon *had* to make sure that his dog obeyed him; there were some battles he had to win and the first one was to stop Devon chasing after cars: the little dog's life might depend on it . . .

Over the weeks Jon tried everything he could think of to get Devon under control. He used his voice and body language to show Devon that he was more powerful – doing big grizzly bear impressions that Julius and Stanley clearly thought were stupid! Devon needed to realize that he must pay attention. But the collie was still proud, still wilful, still independent. And all his instincts still told him to chase and to herd rather than listen to Jon.

Trying to get Devon's attention one day, Jon

suddenly had a brilliant idea: he knew how the dog could chase his cars without being in any danger at all . . .

In the park where he had been brushing Devon there was a fence that ran parallel to a busy street. It was a sturdy, tall, chain-link fence which Devon couldn't get through. Jon led the dog to a point near the fence and watched with interest. Devon did exactly as Jon thought he would. As soon as a lorry or car whizzed along the road, he dropped down into the classic Border collie herding position, tail down, eyes locked on Jon for some kind of command . . .

"Go get 'em!" he yelled.

And Devon was off! He shot towards the fence like a rocket, then veered right to run alongside it. He ran all the way along, chasing the car right to the very end, barking all the way. Then he raced back towards Jon.

He loved it and didn't want to stop. After half a dozen runs up and down the fence, his chest was heaving and his tongue was dangling out of his mouth – but if a dog could smile, then Devon was definitely grinning!

When they got back home, Jon grinned too – Devon had worn himself out for the first time since he'd arrived! He stretched out lazily in the sun next to the Labs and dozed in the back garden – Jon seemed to have found a way for Devon to let off some steam while keeping safe.

Soon Devon wanted to herd the traffic like this every day!

One morning when they were in the park, Jon overheard someone say, "That dog runs so fast!" When he looked round, he saw the boy who had spoken, but he wasn't the only one standing watching: it looked like Devon had a fan club! There was a whole group of people – adults, kids, other dog-owners and people just enjoying the sunshine in the park – who had gathered together to see Devon run. One kid called him "Speedy" and carried a stopwatch! Jon couldn't believe the attention his dog was getting.

From time to time Julius and Stanley came to

the park with Jon and Devon. They sniffed around, licking any children that were about, then just dozed in the sun – as usual the complete opposite to Devon! The collie was constantly working, chasing and herding his prey from safety here in the park.

Clever little Devon quickly seemed to understand that although he could chase the cars like this in the park, Jon got cross with him when he did it anywhere else. Slowly but surely he stopped trying to dash down the street after buses, and Jon began to stop worrying as Devon happily padded along beside him.

He couldn't believe they'd achieved such a breakthrough – he was so pleased with the little dog. Devon had not been with Jon for very long and he knew they still had a long way to go to make sure he really belonged, but he'd had an idea . . . Perhaps they needed to find a peaceful place where they could both relax, wander around without worrying about traffic and build some real trust and affection.

"Who wants a holiday, boys?" he said to all three dogs. Jon decided that it was time to head for the mountains.

CHAPTER SEVEN

Four Musketeers

Most dogs Jon knew loved travelling in cars. They would stick their head out of the windows and let the wind blow into their face, flattening their ears back. He knew that it wasn't really a good idea to let his dogs do this – insects and small stones could easily have hit them in the face or eyes and it could be really dangerous if another car came too close. But when they were driving along towards Jon's cabin in the mountains and he looked back to see Devon's handsome head just outside the rear window, with his nose pointing into the wind like an ice-breaker slicing through Arctic seas, he just didn't have the heart to spoil the little dog's fun.

Jon turned back to concentrate on the road ahead. About halfway into the four-hour drive, he started to relax, thinking about the great holiday they were going to have. Suddenly he heard a furious clawing from behind him . . .

He quickly looked round and his smile froze on his face. Devon was wriggling out through the half-open window! His head and front paws were hanging outside the car – and there were huge trucks rumbling past in the other direction! "Devon, no!" Jon screamed in shock. If the dog got any further, he would fall out into the path of the oncoming traffic – he had to stop him *now*.

Devon jumped at Jon's shout and, realizing he had been naughty, scrabbled to try and get back into the car, but he was stuck. Jon knew he had to do something immediately. He tried to steer the car with one hand, reaching back with the other to grab Devon by his tail.

Julius and Stanley didn't help at all as Jon tried desperately to pull the collie back into the car. They were snoozing away happily, totally ignoring all the fuss and noise!

When Jon finally managed to get the little dog to safety again, he shut all the windows firmly and shook his head. He knew Devon would try it again immediately if he left them open, in spite of the danger and in spite of Jon's anger!

Devon actually didn't seem to mind being shut in – perhaps he had scared himself – and he finally settled down. He foraged around and spotted Jon's lunch lying in a paper bag on the back seat. The cheeky dog then spent the next five minutes removing the ham from the sandwiches and gobbling it down hungrily!

Finally, two long hours later, Jon, Julius, Stanley and Devon arrived safely at the Katz's holiday home up in the mountains. It was a beautiful place

– a big wooden cabin that sat high up at the end of a steep track. Meadows and woods lay all around it and it was a fabulous peaceful place for the dogs to explore. Julius and Stanley had been there many times before with Jon, and they loved it. They spent hours roaming through the woods, chasing balls into lakes and streams, or just staring out at the view, watching the hawks circling in the sky or a spectacular sunrise. It really was a doggy paradise!

As they all got out of the car, Jon wondered what Devon would make of his cabin and how he would behave there. It was all very familiar to Jon and the Labradors, and they had many happy holiday memories – of being lost together, or being caught out in thunderstorms, or curling up in front of the brick fireplace on chilly nights. Their adventures had always just been about the three of them, like the loyal musketeers. Jon crossed his fingers: he hoped they could become the *four* musketeers.

And at first they were. For the first couple of days Devon fitted in perfectly, exploring the quiet hillsides with Jon and the two Labradors and happily racing after a chipmunk or two.

But when, after a few days in the mountains, Jon had to go into the nearby town for some supplies and needed leave the dogs behind, he realized he might have a problem. He didn't like shutting the dogs in when he was at home in the city, but it seemed even more terrible here, where it was so beautiful and peaceful. Julius and Stanley had always stayed by the cabin when Jon told them to. There were no other buildings around, barely any cars on the road, and the dogs liked to hang around just outside the cabin. Devon had been much better while they'd been up here – *Surely he'll stay with the other two dogs*, Jon thought. *I'll only be gone for a short while.* Then he remembered Devon trying to crawl out of the car window on the way there . . .

He didn't want to take any risks – it would be *awful* to lose Devon here in the mountains – so he set a trap for the little Border collie. He left the three dogs on the porch, giving lots of elaborate "stay" commands and hand signals. *Even the daftest*

71

dog would understand what I want them to do! thought Jon, and the way Stanley and Julius looked at him showed that they agreed! Devon looked as though he was planning on staying, as Jon had asked, so he got into his car and drove off.

A hundred metres down the drive, he turned off the car's engine, crept out and crawled on his hands and knees back up the slope. If anybody had seen him, he would've been very embarrassed – he looked ridiculous! Everything was very quiet and still – until Jon suddenly spotted a furry black-and-white shape crawling right above him. It hid in the bushes, moving almost silently. Devon! His trap had worked!

"No! Bad dog! Stay! Get back!" Jon leaped out at the young dog, shouting commands. Devon tore back towards the house with Jon running after him.

Julius and Stanley looked up, puzzled, as their master returned. Their eyes were worried – why was Jon so angry? *They* hadn't done anything wrong.

Devon looked guilty and hung his head as though he knew he'd been naughty. But Jon knew from past experience that this didn't mean he understood that he must stay behind! Further tests were needed. "Stay, Devon. Stay with Julius and Stanley. Good dog . . ." he told the Border collie again.

He drove away from the cabin once more, stopping the car in exactly the same place, and waited to see if Devon was following him. There was no sign of him. Great! Jon drove back to the cabin; Devon was *exactly* where he had left him. Jon went through all this once more – just to be on the safe side – but he was overjoyed to find Devon still in the same place. "Good dog, Devon! Well done, boy."

Jon was pleased. It really did seem as though they had made some progress and Devon had learned his lesson: he must know now that it was not safe for him to run off alone. Jon drove off happily.

He was actually away from the cabin for a very short time – it was no more than ten minutes before he was heading home again. At the bottom of the mountain, as he approached the track that led to the cabin, Jon smiled. He thought of everything he had gone through with Devon so far – it was a relief to know that he was paying attention and was safe up at the cabin with Julius and Stanley.

As these thoughts passed through Jon's head, he suddenly spotted a familiar sleek black-and-white head peeping out from behind a barn. Devon!

Once the little dog had realized that Jon had really left and wasn't just setting one of his traps, he'd followed the car all the way down the mountain – over a mile – and was now waiting for Jon to return!

"Devon!" Jon roared, slamming on his brakes and jumping out of the car. "Come here now!"

There was a flash of movement and a blur of black and white as the little dog disappeared into the trees – *away* from Jon, not towards him! Back in the car, with his car tyres kicking up clouds of dust, Jon zoomed along the road as fast as he could after the dog and veered onto the track. Where was Devon? Was he back home? Or was he now roaming around the mountainside?

Jon worked himself up into a panic, but when he climbed out of the car, Devon was sitting on the porch with Julius and Stanley. All three of their tails wagged happily; at first glance they looked as though they hadn't moved an inch in all the time Jon had been away, but as he stared at Devon, he saw that he was panting heavily!

This incident with Devon decided it for Jon – the next time he went off without them he would have to shut all three dogs inside the cabin. They would still have plenty of chances to run around in the garden and in and out of the house while Jon was there.

The next day they did just this: Jon was indoors working on his new book, and every now and then he would look up to see Devon, Julius and Stanley wandering in and out of the door just as they wished. It was so peaceful that he became more and more engrossed in his work . . . After ten minutes he looked up, shaking his head as he brought himself back to the real world. He glanced around to check on the dogs.

Julius and Stanley were dozing as usual . . . But Devon had disappeared!

Jon called out for him, but there was no answering bark. He rushed outside, his heart thumping, to check the nearest meadow and the drive. There was no sign of the dog. Panicking now, Jon ran back and forth through the woods, shouting Devon's name, but there was no answer.

He was terrified. Jon knew from seeing Devon chase his car that the Border collie knew his way down the mountain and back up again. But there was so much space up here – lots of woods to explore and very few people around. A frightened dog could easily get himself lost. And if he was still out by the time it got dark, he'd be scared to death and completely alone . . .

Jon pulled himself together and called the sheriff, the local animal warden and the nearest vet to report Devon missing. He also phoned all his nearest neighbours before beginning to search further afield. He drove up and down the mountain, shouting Devon's name out of the window. Surely he would come when he saw the car, Jon kept telling himself. He loved to chase cars so much. If he hadn't been so worried, Jon would have laughed at himself – for the first time ever, he actually *wanted* Devon to chase his car!

"Devon, where are you?" he shouted. "Good dog! Good dog! Come here, Devon . . ." But after three hours there was still no sign of the little collie.

By this time, Jon was hot and exhausted and had almost given up hope of finding Devon that day. Wearily he went back to his cabin, calling out one last time before he went inside. Suddenly there was a rustle from the woods, and Devon exploded out from them! He was covered in burrs and mud, but he was overjoyed to see Jon. His tail wagged furiously, and he leaped into the air, licking Jon's face, barking and whining. He had never looked happier!

Jon was just too happy to have Devon back to be cross with him, and Devon was just as happy to be back, even running over to Julius and Stanley to lick them lovingly. He didn't leave Jon's side for the rest of the day. Sometimes you have to be away from home to work out what home really means, and Devon had just worked out that "home" for him meant Jon.

Jon hugged Devon fiercely to him. He knew then how much he loved the troublesome young Border collie. Devon was here to stay, whatever he had in store for his master – and Jon suspected there was still a *lot* of trouble to come.

CHAPTER EIGHT

Showdown

Back home, where there was traffic and noise and danger, there were problems. Jon tried everything he knew – and everything he'd learned when he was training Julius and Stanley – to try and get Devon to behave like a good dog all the time.

Devon *was* trying, but it didn't always work . . .

During the weeks after they returned from their holiday, Devon:

- Jumped on the tables in the house, knocking things over. (The whole house now had to be organized around him, or all Jon's favourite things would soon be broken. Jon's wife, Paula, was very understanding, but there was no doubt that Devon could make an awful mess when he tried!)
- Threw himself against one of the stained-glass panels by the front door so hard that he broke the glass and bent the lead out of shape.
- Grabbed Stanley's bed, stealing his rawhide chews and pinching his favourite spot in the living room.
- Refused to walk properly on a lead. He just pulled ahead as hard as he could. Jon found it harder and harder to walk all three dogs together. Devon jumped out at buses and lorries, sometimes even pulling Jon right over.
- Wouldn't sit, lie down, stay or do *anything* Jon asked him to do.

After his experience in the woods, Devon now wanted to be with Jon all the time: he tried to go with his master whenever he went out and he loved to jump up into his arms for a big hug. Jon loved this too, but he was beginning to feel desperate. Devon was very affectionate, but he was also stubborn. He just *would not* do as he was told.

Eventually Jon phoned Deanne, the lady who had bred Devon, to ask her for help.

"Devon's like his mother," she told him. "Very headstrong and wilful." This didn't surprise Jon. But what Deanne went on to say next made him worry: "You can't keep a dog who's behaving like this. You have to convince him that you're in charge, and you're not going to abandon him, or you might not be able to keep him."

Jon was devastated. He really thought that he and Devon had been getting somewhere – all that work in the park and in the mountains seemed to have come to nothing, and now Deanne was telling him that if he wasn't up to the job, it might be fairer to everyone – including Devon – if the dog went back to her and she tried to find him a new home.

But this made Jon even more determined to break through Devon's barriers, train him and become his friend and master. He just couldn't send him back – put him into a box again and watch him fly away. He *loved* the little dog – even if he *was* the naughtiest dog in the world. He and Devon had been through so much together already, Jon didn't want to imagine how awful – and how boring! – it would be not to have Devon in his life any more.

Jon knew that no owner should give up on a dog before trying everything to make it work first. That's what had happened with Devon's last owners, and Jon was determined to be different. "I'd like to try everything possible," he told Deanne, "before I even *think* of giving him up."

Deanne was happy to hear it. "You can do this," she told Jon encouragingly, "but I should warn you, it's going to be tough – a real battle of wills!"

It was a battle that Jon *had* to win. There could be only one leader in the pack and that had to be Jon, not Devon.

"When Devon accepts you as his leader," Deanne told him, "he will roll over on his back and show you his belly. That's the gesture of submission. If he does that, you've won."

Determined to prove to Deanne that he could make things work, Jon went out and bought a shorter lead and two choke chains – one to put around Devon's neck, and one to throw around and make a noise with while he was training the young Border collie. This was it for Jon: the battle to train Devon was now really going to begin!

Devon seemed to know this, and being the clever, stubborn dog he was, he tried just as hard as Jon to win, often doing the very opposite of what his new master wanted him to do. When Jon asked Devon to sit and he didn't, Jon would throw the choke chain at his feet to make a noise and then he would press his hand down on Devon's rump to *make* him sit. He spent hours working with Devon, determined to make him finally accept him as his boss.

It didn't work. Devon hated this kind of training

and was getting more and more disobedient, staring at Jon with a challenging look in his eyes. It was as if he was determined not to give in. He would *not* do what he was told and Jon was getting more and more miserable about it.

One day Jon took Devon out alone for an early morning walk when he thought it would be quiet. For a few steps Devon padded along obediently beside Jon. *Phew!* he thought, leaning over to pat the dog to say well done. But as he did so, Devon spotted a small minibus. Exactly as he had done all those weeks ago, he pulled the lead right out of Jon's hand and leaped in front of the bus. The driver slammed on his brakes, the tyres screeched, and a couple of kids on the bus screamed loudly.

"No! No! Bad dog!" Jon was furious! He grabbed Devon by the scruff of his neck, dragging him back onto the pavement, and tried to apologize to the bus driver.

Devon was a clever dog, and he'd been with Jon long enough to know perfectly well that he wasn't allowed to run into the road. Ever since the collie had first arrived, Jon had made that very clear – every single day; ten times every single day! He couldn't understand why Devon was now ignoring all his training. Why was he *deliberately* doing something he knew would make Jon angry?

Jon forced himself to calm down – getting cross with Devon like this wasn't going to help either of them – and they continued on their way. Devon walked quietly next to Jon again, as if thinking about what his master had just said to him. But then, a few minutes later, he did exactly the same thing again! This time he tore free of his lead to chase after an even bigger, louder bus than before, then threw himself at the front tyres. Jon was terrified! As the bus passed by, Devon barked and jumped back – only just missing being hit. The little Border collie could very easily have been killed and it seemed as though he was only doing it to annoy Jon.

Jon snapped. This *could not* go on.

He was so angry that he wasn't thinking clearly: he grabbed Devon, one hand on his collar, the other on his haunches, and hurled him onto the grassy strip next to the kerb. Devon landed on his feet, darted away and then stood his ground. He looked as if he wasn't going to back down.

Jon was so cross that he was struggling to control himself. He threw the metal poop-scoop, meaning for it to hit the pavement and make a clanging noise, but it hit Devon in the shoulder. The dog didn't even blink. Jon screamed with anger. "Don't you understand?!" he bellowed in rage. "If I can't get you to obey me, I can't keep you safe – so I won't be able to keep you!" He had never lost his temper like this before.

He was interrupted in his ranting by a car pulling up beside them. A middle-aged woman was driving and she had a young girl with her. The woman rolled down the window and looked snootily at Jon. "Excuse me, but my daughter doesn't like the way you are treating your dog," she told him.

Jon could hardly believe his ears; he was outraged. His house was full of special food for the dogs, there were dog beds everywhere, collections of dog toys and balls . . . He was the man who had once dived into swollen flood waters to rescue Stanley from being washed away; the man who had lain down in the street with his arm down a drain to retrieve his dog's favourite ball. In short, he was the kind of dog owner any dog would *love* to live with. "Mind your own business!" he told her angrily.

Of *course* Jon wasn't pleased with the way he was behaving right at this moment. He had never shouted at a dog like that before in his whole life – and he knew it wasn't right to try and bully Devon into doing what he was told, but he was desperate. The collie had nearly been hit by a bus simply because he refused to obey Jon, refused to accept him as his leader. The woman was right: Jon shouldn't have lost his temper, but he would like to see *her* try and get Devon to do what he was told!

The woman rolled up the car window and drove off in a huff. Jon turned back towards Devon . . . and his jaw dropped. The little Border collie was lying on his back, feet in the air, his ears so far back they were nearly flat against his head. Just as Deanne had predicted, he had submitted; he had acknowledged that Jon was his master.

Devon had made his decision. He had fought long and hard, and had not given in easily. But now he'd decided he was surrendering. For such a proud little dog to act like this was a powerful demonstration of his trust in Jon – who couldn't believe his eyes. After all this time and all this effort, Devon was finally admitting that he trusted Jon. Now Jon had to show Devon that he deserved that trust.

Jon wiped his head, so relieved. Shouting at Devon could so easily have been an awful mistake – he felt terrible about his behaviour – but in this case it seemed to have worked. He approached Devon slowly, knelt down by his side, and turned him over so he was no longer on his back. The young dog crawled onto his lap, his head resting in his arms. Pressing his face close to Jon's, he licked him tentatively – once, twice, then a hundred times! His tail began to swish.

"It's OK, boy," Jon told him gently, now feeling

guilty for his outburst. "I love you. You're home. You're home for good. And I'll never abandon you, I promise." He stroked Devon's head and neck. "I won't shout at you like that again, ever. And I promise you," he continued, knowing how much the little dog had had to give up to behave as he wanted him to, "we'll go and find some real sheep as soon as things settle down, and you can herd them."

People stared at them as they passed – the man and the little Border collie sitting together on the pavement. But Jon and Devon ignored everybody – they had finally made friends.

CHAPTER NINE

Lots and Lots of Heart

Now that Devon had decided to give Jon all his trust and love, Jon began to discover just how much the little dog had to give. The war was over and Devon had definitely accepted Jon as his leader, paying him more attention than ever before. In fact the little dog seemed fascinated by his master. He kept him in sight at all times now, sitting at the door of whatever room he was in so that he could keep an eye on him!

Soon their friendship and partnership became so

close that Devon even seemed to know what Jon was thinking, what he wanted him to do and where he wanted him to go. Jon had a bad leg from an old injury, which sometimes played up and caused him a lot of pain; when this happened, Devon seemed to know straight away. If Jon ever stumbled or tripped, the dog moved instantly to his side with a worried look in his eyes, and licked his hand. Jon felt certain that if he ever fell over and needed real help, he would only have to shout, "Devon, go on. Get help!" and the little Border collie would know exactly what to do – rush off and fetch someone.

"Good dog, Devon! Good dog!" Jon now said many times a day – meaning it every time!

Devon no longer ran away or darted into the street. He could even walk off the lead!

He stopped chasing buses, or nipping at people's heels.

He didn't try and jump the fence any more, or dig holes under it.

He ate from his own bowl, leaving Stanley's alone.

Yet he kept all his spirit and pride. He was a working dog now – and a very clever one – and he held his beautiful head high. Underneath all the mischief-making, all the disobedience, Devon had an affectionate nature: it was now clear to everyone that he was a dog with lots and lots of heart.

Devon clearly loved Jon more than anything, and it wasn't long before Jon needed Devon's love and support more than ever . . .

During their daily walks, Jon began to notice that Stanley, the younger of the two Labradors, was lagging way behind Julius and Devon and that there was a sad look in his eyes.

After some weeks of this, Jon decided to take Stanley to the vet. He didn't seem to mind: he was perfectly happy to go along to the surgery in his crate, nuzzling Dr Brenda King hello when they entered and trotting along beside her to the X-ray machine. Dr King smiled down at him – she'd always had a soft spot for Stanley.

But when she returned, her smile was gone. She

closed her office door, leaving Stanley in the test room, and sat down in front of Jon. Jon panicked; it must be bad news if Dr King didn't want to say it in front of the Lab. He was right.

"I'm sorry . . ." she said to Jon, with a sad look in her eyes. Her tests had shown that Stanley had a big problem with his heart; it was slowing down, which was why he had seemed so tired. The X-ray had also shown that his hips were causing problems too – it was becoming more and more painful for him to walk. Soon he would be completely crippled. "I'm surprised he can even chase the ball," Dr King said sadly.

Jon closed his eyes. He knew that Stanley would chase his ball with his last breath – it was absolutely his favourite game, even if it caused him pain.

Jon thought a lot about Stanley and what Dr King had told him. Stanley's heart was failing, and unless Jon agreed for the dog to have a huge operation, or to be put on medication that would make him even sicker, there was nothing Dr King could do to make him better. Jon didn't know what to do.

When he took Stanley in for another test a little while later, he talked about his dog with Dr King. Stanley was already getting much worse: he had lost most of his energy and was completely exhausted on long walks. "What you've got to do," the vet told him, "is work out what the best thing is for Stanley. Nobody else can do that."

And Jon knew that she was right. *What would Stanley want?* he asked himself. He knew the answer, though he had never been sadder about anything in his life. Stanley would want to end his life as happily as he had lived it. He would hate not to be able to walk, or chase his ball, or walk alongside Jon and Julius and Devon. Jon loved Stanley so much and there was no way he wanted him to be in pain all the time and not to have fun.

After a lot of thought, and with great sadness, Jon finally spoke to Dr King: "Stanley has been happy every day of his life. I don't want that to change." It was a horrible decision – but Jon agreed to have Stanley put down. He would miss his dog so much – miss his morning cuddles, his beautiful face and his happy, fun-loving nature, but he was only brave enough to make this decision because he was sure it was right for Stanley.

As if he sensed that Jon was upset, Stanley padded across the vet's office and put his head between his master's knees, his tail wagging as he tried to cheer him up. Jon gulped back a tear. He knew there and then that he had made the right decision.

Jon wanted to say goodbye to Stanley properly and give him the perfect last holiday, so he decided to take all three dogs up into the mountains again.

While they were there, he cooked Stanley a sirloin steak for his dinner and gently threw him his favourite mangled blue ball. Then they went out for a gentle stroll in Stanley's favourite bit of the woods. Julius and Devon hung back a little, letting Jon walk alongside Stanley, just the two of them. It was as if they all knew what was going to happen when they got home.

Four days later, after their return, Jon took Stanley to the vet and said goodbye for ever. "I love you, pal. I love you," he cried as Stanley fell asleep for the last time.

When he got home, Devon and Julius were ready to help him through the loss. They sensed how sad Jon was, and tried their best to comfort him, snuggling close and licking his hand. Jon patted them both on the head – he knew how lucky he was.

CHAPTER TEN

"Go, Devon, Go!"

Once the summer was over, and Jon and Paula and Julius and Devon were getting used to life without Stanley, things looked like they were going to change again.

Out of the blue, Jon was offered a month's work teaching in a university away from home. It would mean moving nearly two thousand miles away to Minneapolis, and living in a university flat without his wife. There was a lot to think about – Devon most of all!

"I can't do it," Jon told the university at first. "I have this new dog, a Border collie. He's a rescue dog and I can't leave him yet. He is just beginning to believe that he is safe with me."

The university weren't sure about Jon bringing a pet with him. But there was no way he was going without Devon – he'd just got the little dog to trust him; he couldn't leave him alone for weeks now. "I have a bad leg and fall over a lot," Jon insisted. "Devon's job is to steer me away from holes and rough bits on the pavement."

The university were keen for Jon to work for them and they seemed to understand that if they didn't let Devon come, then Jon wouldn't come either. They agreed to find Jon an apartment that allowed dogs and get him special permission to take Devon with him to his classes. "Bring him along!" they told Jon eventually.

Jon knew that Julius would hate to move homes, even for just a short time. He would be much happier staying where things were familiar and Paula and Emma and their friends could make sure he didn't miss out on walks or hugs. So it was only one dog bed that Jon packed into the back of his car some weeks later as he got ready to set off for his temporary new home.

It took days to reach the university by car, but Jon and Devon had a great time! Remembering the last time he and Devon had taken a long trip together, Jon made sure all the windows in the car were closed, but to his surprise Devon was very well behaved. He slept on his dog bed from time to time, and occasionally came forward to rest his head on Jon's shoulder, gazing at the road ahead as if he was concentrating very hard to help his master find the way.

Devon liked running about when they stopped for a break, and it was during these rest stops that Jon learned something new about Devon . . . He loved McDonald's! Whenever they were ready to eat, Jon would tie Devon's lead to an outdoor picnic table from where they could still see each other, go inside and order some food for them both. Devon's favourite was a Quarter Pounder with cheese and French fries, but he was also quite keen on Egg McMuffins for breakfast!

The block of flats the university had found for Jon turned out to be full of dogs. It was as if almost everyone in Minneapolis who had a dog lived there. When they finally arrived after their long journey, Jon and Devon were surprised to see poodles and German shepherds, pointers, little yippy terriers, even other Border collies all woofing and whining in a huge doggy chorus. And they were all over the place – dozing on balconies, barking through doors, being walked around the grounds. They found that there was even a huge lake nearby – Devon would love that – and, even better, a park!

Jon was amazed by how quickly and easily Devon adapted to their new routine. And as long as he was with Jon, the little collie was happy. Wherever Jon went, he went! In the morning Jon would drive over to the university, tie Devon up outside the café and get a takeaway breakfast.

"He's gorgeous!"

"Say hello to this fabulous dog."

"What a lovely Border collie!" people would say, and sometimes a whole queue would form, just to give Devon a hug or a kiss. He loved the attention, tossing his head proudly and looking through the café window to make sure Jon noticed him too. The collie had a fan club!

Soon Devon became the café mascot. The owner told Jon to bring him inside, and Devon would go from table to table, saying hello to everyone, holding up a paw and happily accepting little treats.

At the university he even joined Jon in the classroom. He would sink to the floor and fall asleep as soon as his master began teaching. "I hope my students pay more attention, boy!" Jon laughed one day as Devon crunched down one of the dog biscuits the students often bought for him.

At lunch time they took a walk around the park and along the banks of the Mississippi river, before going back to the office, where Devon would curl up on his dog bed.

Devon couldn't believe his luck. He was with Jon every minute of every day. And Jon began to love having him there too. They missed Paula, Emma and Julius, but they made a great team and took good care of each other.

Devon loved living in this new place – there were all sorts of new things to see and do. He had many admirers and got lots of attention, but his favourite new activity was chasing the slow, overfed squirrels that lived around the university! But squirrels were not the only wildlife Devon was to meet in Minneapolis . . .

During their second week he and Jon were walking around the nearby park when a group of people came up to them. "Is your dog a Border collie?" they asked Jon. When he told them he was, they said, "We've heard that Border collies can chase geese away." Jon looked at them, puzzled, so they explained why they were so interested. Their children loved playing football but they couldn't at the moment because the nearby pitch was always covered with nasty goose mess. Sometimes there were so many geese there that the children couldn't even get onto the pitch!

The geese in the Minneapolis area were fat and lazy. Many of them no longer bothered to fly south in the cold winter months, since there was so much tasty rubbish left around by humans. And wherever there were geese, there were smelly droppings too.

Jon was intrigued; Devon looked up as the people talked to his master, as though he was interested in what they were saying. Jon wondered if Devon's instincts could serve some useful purpose here. Chasing geese would be far safer for him than chasing buses.

The very next morning he and Devon headed for the football pitch, where the children were waiting impatiently to start their game. Waddling around and honking about fifty metres in front of them were . . . about two hundred geese!

Jon wasn't totally sure that Devon would know what to do – the little dog looked puzzled by these noisy creatures in front of him. But as soon as one of the kids started to cheer him on – "Go, Devon, go!" – he got the idea and dropped into his stalking position, crouched low with his head almost on the ground, ready to spring forward.

Jon was interested to see if his dog could do it. "You ready? You ready?" he called enthusiastically.

"Yeah! Go, Devon," one of the football coaches called.

The geese begin to honk louder.

Devon crouched even lower, desperate to herd something and work off some energy. He looked up at Jon; he wasn't sure what his master wanted him to do – and actually Jon wasn't really sure, either, but this was a matter of pride now. Devon had to show everyone how clever Border collies were.

"Good boy," Jon said, his hand in the air. Then he brought his arm down and yelled, "Devon, *GO GET 'EM!*"

Almost before the words had left Jon's mouth, Devon was off, racing down the field, kicking up puffs of grass behind him as he went.

He circled the flock, crouching down low, and the geese turned to face him, two of them stepping forward, prepared to do battle.

Devon barked madly now: how dare these creatures ignore him!

He charged,

nipped,

darted behind the two geese leaders,

turned and lunged at the others.

He was like a black-and-white missile hurling himself at the geese, and as he barked and snapped furiously, the geese started to pay attention.

There was a flapping and a honking, and then a great *whoosh* as the geese lifted off from the football pitch, heading for the skies.

"Yeah, Devon! Attaboy, Devon!" The crowd of kids and parents and coaches all cheered loudly before running over to shower Devon with hugs and kisses.

Devon was triumphant! He was a credit to his breed: his tail wagged, his ears pricked up, his chest puffed out – he was one very proud dog!

CHAPTER ELEVEN

A New Friend Arrives . . . And Another Leaves

Jon still often spoke to Deanne, Devon's breeder – she was very interested in Devon's progress and loved to hear what he had been up to! One day while Jon and Devon were still living at the university she called up – Jon now recognized her tone of voice. "I have a puppy for you . . ." Deanne told him. She had a new litter of Border collies, Devon's cousins, and it apparently included one of the sweetest, most lovable puppies she had ever seen. But as she explained to Jon, he had a slight problem with his eyes, meaning that he wouldn't be suitable for a show home and she'd have trouble selling him.

"He'd make a perfect companion dog for Devon," she told Jon. "I know you've got your hands full, but he's so sweet. He won't want to be the boss. He'll play with Devon, but he'll never try and take over the number one spot from him. Just think about it . . . Why don't I send you a photo so you can see what he looks like?"

As soon as the photograph arrived, Jon's heart melted. He stared down at a beautiful fuzzy little bright-eyed face. *Homer*, Jon thought. *He looks like a Homer.* "That's not fair," he told Deanne. "That dog is totally adorable. How can you do this to me again? Think of Devon and Julius."

"Don't take him if you're not ready . . . seriously." Deanne laughed. "But I think he'd be fantastic for you."

Jon thought hard about what Deanne had said.

Julius was a very happy and secure dog. He knew that he and Jon had a great relationship and he had never felt threatened by Devon so Jon didn't think a docile little puppy would be a problem for him. *But what about Devon?* Jon had spent so long making things right for him and getting Devon to trust him. He didn't want it all to be disrupted by a new dog. But the more he thought about it, the more he could see that inviting another Border collie into his home might be a good idea. The two collies could exercise each other: Jon was always trying to wear Devon out, but mostly it worked the other way round! Apparently Homer was a very happy, fun-loving dog. Jon could picture the two collies playing together, digging holes together, chasing things together, and Devon could help train him . . . They could become best mates. It could be good for everybody.

Back home, he showed the photograph of Homer to Paula – she was immediately won over by the puppy's sweet little face, just like Jon had been! Three short weeks later, Jon found himself driving to the airport to meet Homer!

Remembering his experiences with Devon, he had asked Deanne to have Homer sent to a much quieter airport, and she had happily agreed.

Jon took Devon to the airport with him – really he had no choice; Devon still rarely left his side! – but he left him waiting on the back seat of the car while he went in to collect the new guy.

As Homer's plastic dog crate was wheeled over into the baggage area a few minutes later, Jon crossed his fingers, hoping it would be easier to get Homer home than it had been Devon. He needn't have worried. He heard two of the baggage handlers cooing over the little puppy as they came closer. "He's *so* sweet," one of them told Jon as they handed him over. "He's been trying to lick us . . ."

Jon opened the crate – just a crack! – and eased his hand in. Homer edged away, shaking. Something about Jon had frightened him. He was smaller, thinner and more awkward than Devon had been, but very, very cute! He still had all his brown-grey puppy fuzz.

Jon lifted up the terrified little puppy and carried him out to the car. Though Homer was obviously very frightened, when Jon looked into his eyes he saw that he was taking in everything around him. He gazed about at every sight and sound, his head tilting first to one side, then to the other. He was very trusting and calm, happy to let Jon carry him. Jon couldn't help comparing it to Devon's arrival nearly a year earlier, and now these two very different puppies were about to meet for the first time!

Devon wasn't usually all that interested in other dogs. Once he realized that they weren't something he could herd, he tended not to pay them any attention. He was a tireless furry ball of energy, but Jon had never known him be aggressive towards another animal. So he couldn't believe it when he opened the car door to introduce the two Border collies and Devon started snarling viciously – and attacked Homer! He suddenly had the little puppy on the ground, going for his throat. Homer squealed in terror.

Jon was shocked and outraged and he quickly pushed Devon off the yapping Homer. Devon stared back at his master defiantly and it was suddenly obvious to Jon what he was thinking: *I know what you're up to, but I don't want this runt in our car, our house, our lives. There's no room for* him.

"This dog," Jon hissed crossly at Devon, "is coming to live with us. *Leave him alone!*"

Devon glowered angrily from the back seat. He kept his dark eyes on Homer all the way home, watching him like a hawk and growling threateningly every now and then. Homer curled up into a ball on the passenger seat, snuggling close to Jon for protection and nibbling on some little biscuits. Jon looked down – Homer was such an adorable little bundle of fluff! he thought.

When they arrived home, Jon quickly let the two dogs out of the car, but Devon immediately lunged at Homer's head again, making both Homer and Jon scream out.

Disturbed by the noise, Julius ambled over to see what was interupting his peace, and, in contrast to Devon, greeted Homer by licking him affectionately. Homer looked up at the older dog with amazement and seemed to love Julius immediately, padding happily along behind him.

Devon watched the other two dogs angrily, looking up at Jon from time to time too. He couldn't quite believe that his master could betray him by bringing another Border collie back home with him. He paced up and down outside the living room, where Jon, Julius and Homer now gathered, his eyes never once leaving the little puppy. But Jon ignored the grumpy dog. "This is your new home, boy," he told Homer. "You are going to be so happy with us all." He sat down on the carpet and waited for a moment. Homer – so sweet! – crawled carefully into his lap and gently licked his hand. Jon grinned, scratching the puppy's tummy and feeding him some biscuits. Julius stood over the new arrival as if protecting him from this new moody Devon.

Dog Report: First Impressions

Name: *Homer*

Age: *16 weeks*

Breed: *Border collie; he's a brown-grey colour that breeders call "blue"*

Looks: *Covered in cute puppy fuzz, he looks like a small fox, with bright, curious eyes (Devon looked more like a wolf when he arrived)*

Personality: *Lovable little bundle of fluff. He adores everybody, especially Julius*

Jon's challenge: *Devon has to accept that Homer is part of our family; and he has to share the attention. Homer has to be trained too, so I need to spend lots of time with him without upsetting Devon*

Homer may have been the same breed as Devon, but he could not have been more different. While Devon liked to have an argument and Jon had to prove to him that he was a boss he could trust, Homer wanted no trouble at all. All he needed to know was what Jon wanted so he could do it – and how to avoid annoying Devon!

Jon began by training Homer in the garden for just fifteen minutes a day. They worked in the front garden at first, until Jon noticed that Homer kept looking uneasily at the house. When Jon followed the puppy's gaze, he saw a pair of dark eyes glowering at them from an upstairs window – Devon!

It put them both off, so the next day Jon decided to take Homer to the park instead. When they returned, Jon knew straight away that Devon had left him a message. There were a couple of forks on the settee; his shoes were now in a pile (the laces carefully removed); and a pile of cushions lay in the middle of the room. Nothing was destroyed or damaged, but Jon knew exactly what Devon was saying to him: *Leave me behind and I'll make you pay* . . .

And for the next few days, every time Jon took Homer out, this was what happened. Introducing Homer into his home was not proving as easy as Jon had hoped.

Just like Devon, Homer liked to keep Jon in sight, moving from room to room with him, and he wriggled and squealed with joy if Jon patted or hugged him, loving the attention. But Devon had scared the puppy badly: he wouldn't go and sit beside Jon if the older Border collie was about for fear of what Devon would do to him.

Devon was absolutely the dominant dog, now the number two in the pack after Jon, and he wanted to keep it that way. He missed the attention and Jon was struggling to know how to deal with his bad-tempered dog.

"It's not OK for Devon to keep Homer away from you," Deanne advised him when he called her for help. "It's *your* job to decide who can approach you."

Jon took a deep breath: he knew this was going to take time, but he'd won Devon round once; he could do it again!

He started to train the two dogs together, hoping that Devon would show the puppy what to do. Homer was clever and he soon learned that when Jon shouted during their training sessions it was normally directed at Devon. He also understood that Jon would protect him from Devon. Slowly he became less scared of the older dog, and Devon began to realize that Homer did not want to take his place in the pack, but simply wanted to be his friend.

Slowly but surely the two dogs grew used to each other. The puppy would pad around behind Devon expectantly – and the day Jon saw Devon give Homer a friendly early morning lick, he whooped in delight.

However, Homer's favourite doggy friend was still Julius, and the two of them seemed like grandfather and grandson. Whenever Devon glowered at Homer or snatched his toys away, the puppy would pad over to Julius and curl up with him for comfort.

Labradors are always very calm dogs, but now Jon noticed that Julius moved around even less than he had before. At first he wondered if the dog was missing his old friend Stanley and feeling sad. Sometimes Jon would take the two collies out for a walk, and when they came back – hours later – Julius had barely moved.

When the Lab did come out on walks now, he lagged way behind, Jon realized, never really wanting to leave the house. Reluctantly he had to admit that something must be very wrong, and with a heavy heart he took Julius to visit Dr King, the vet.

Jon couldn't believe it when he learned the terrible news. Julius was very ill – with a growth that the vet admitted she could not remove or cure. Just as with Stanley, Jon needed to make the same brave decision. And say the same painful goodbye.

After Julius had gone to sleep for the last time

and Jon came home without his much-loved Labrador, he wondered if Julius had gone to a doggy paradise; to a mountaintop where he could lie gazing out over the meadows, a parade of foxes, rabbits and deer passing by for his amusement. But – a special feature just for Julius – there was a river between him and them so he didn't have to chase them and could happily just lie in the sun and watch them. There were children everywhere, to hug and love him. And Stanley would be there too so the old friends would be reunited.

Worried that her dad was missing Julius, Emma called home to see how he was. Jon felt a lump in his throat when he heard his daughter's voice. "There's a big hole in my heart," he told her, staring sadly at Julius's empty dog bed. He would never forget his faithful Labs.

Losing Julius affected Devon and Homer too: they both missed him very much – Homer especially. But they seemed to realize that Jon needed them to support him, so they both tried to comfort him, snuggling up to him. Jon smiled, thinking how lucky he was that he still had Devon and Homer to live with him. These two dogs were the ones he would think about now.

CHAPTER TWELVE

Dog Days

Life began to settle into a new rhythm – days with Devon and Homer were busy and fun, filled with play and work, love and exercise. Jon wrote a lot, walked a lot, got licked a lot, scratched ears a lot, threw balls, and handed out biscuits and a squeaky toy or two.

Most days began the same way:

6.30 a.m.
This is when Jon first opens his eyes. Devon is

always – *always* – sitting on the floor a couple of metres from the bed, watching and waiting. Jon waves a lazy hand and Devon hops quietly onto the bed and puts his head on Jon's shoulder, licks his hand or face, then sighs deeply and goes to sleep.

7.30 a.m.

Paula's alarm clock goes off and Homer sneaks up to the bed on the other side. With a wary look at Devon, he wriggles up and sneaks into any available space. Homer loves to cuddle up to Paula. Sometimes Jon looks across and sees him wrapped around her head like a fluffy turban!

Breakfast

The dogs get their breakfast before Jon and Paula (of course), but then lie in the hall, waiting for the really exciting moment when it's time for . . .

Morning walk

As soon as Jon pushes back his chair, the dogs leap to their feet and head for the back door. *Walkies!*

★ ★ ★

Border collies didn't simply go through doors – they *exploded*. When it was time for their morning walk, the two dogs flew out of the house as if shot from cannons, checking round and round the garden first to make sure nothing had changed overnight, before Jon opened the gate and they all set off.

Both dogs walked off the lead now, listening for Jon's commands, and as they walked along shady streets, in and around parks, along grass verges, zigzagging through the neighbourhood, Jon gave the dogs various instructions, to keep their interest and give them a bit of obedience training. Devon and Homer were both used to these instructions and obeyed them instantly:

"Hey, guys, pay attention!" Jon would point across the street – so they knew where he wanted them to go.

"Let's go, heel" – so they could tear across at high speed.

"Heel slowly" – which meant they had to trot along calmly by his side.

Jon couldn't bear to get rid of Stanley's old blue ball and he still carried it in his pocket whenever he went out. Homer sometimes pushed his nose against him, wanting him to throw the ball. He didn't nip Jon's bottom as Stanley used to, but he loved to chase a ball almost as much – though he wasn't quite as good as Stanley at bringing it back again!

Devon, of course, wanted nothing to do with such a silly game, but if he saw that Homer was having fun without him, he sometimes snatched the ball and brought it over to Jon, just to show that he could *easily* do this trick – he just thought it was beneath him.

Both dogs knew many of their neighbours now, but while Devon wasn't bothered whether or not anyone came over to say hello to him, Homer bounded up to almost everyone they passed, tail going, ready to offer licks. He had heaps of doggy friends now and *woof*ed hello as he passed by their houses. His best friends were:

Zeus – a German shepherd three times his size;

Seamus – a tiny, energetic Westie;

Daisy – a curly-haired retriever;

and Minnie, a deaf bull terrier he had met in the park.

And whenever Homer saw one of them, the two dogs would wrestle around happily in a blurry ball, full of energy and fun!

Devon and Homer went almost everywhere with Jon now. If he had to get his hair cut, buy flowers, pick up dry-cleaning, get a picture framed, browse in the local bookshop – whatever he was doing, Devon and Homer went too. But neither of them minded so much any more when Jon *did* have to leave them alone, as they had each other for company. If Jon was working indoors, he would occasionally glance out of the window and see them sitting side by side in the garden, like two old friends fishing on a river bank.

When they were left alone and free to roam about the house, there were still moments of naughtiness – sometimes Jon would find pillows on the floor and CD cases on the bed – and though he and Paula suspected that Devon was to blame, they never caught him in the act!

After a trip to the cinema one night, Jon and Paula came home to find the fridge door open. *A whole roast chicken* was missing! They didn't have to wonder who was to blame! Naughty Devon was nowhere to be seen . . . And suddenly, out of the corner of his eye, Jon caught sight of Devon's tail as he scurried silently up the stairs. They looked all over the house for the missing chicken; at last Jon saw something under one of the living-room chairs. "Aha!" he cried, spotting the bottom half of the plastic container that held the chicken. But when he looked inside, there was not a bit of chicken remaining! Jon eventually found the rest of the container underneath the sofa – but there was no chicken in that either! He just had no idea how Devon had managed to pull the chicken out of the fridge, carry it nearly eight metres, remove all the wrapping and eat the whole thing without leaving a single trace of it. He had even hidden the two bits of evidence under two different pieces of furniture. He was the cleverest, and naughtiest, dog Jon had ever known!

However, Devon did not manage to get away with it for long. What goes in one end of a dog soon comes out the other, and Jon and Paula soon found out where the chicken had got to – inside Devon's tummy!

Eating chicken bones can be very dangerous for a dog, and Jon felt terrible, blaming himself for not double checking that he'd shut the fridge door properly before he and Paula left for the cinema. He called the vet to check that Devon was OK, and she reassured him, telling him to just keep a close eye on him. Jon decided to wedge a chair in front of the fridge as an extra precaution whenever he and Paula went out.

Two days later, the plate of meatballs Jon had planned to have for his lunch vanished from the fridge. When he went into the kitchen, he saw that the chair was pushed aside and the door ajar. The container the meatballs had been in was hidden under a chair again. Jon felt as if events were repeating themselves, especially when once again he caught Devon edging guiltily towards the stairs!

"No!" Jon charged after Devon. He tripped over the carpet, falling flat on his face, and by the time he'd picked himself up again, Homer was there in front of him, looking terrified, but there was no sign of Devon.

Jon was about to get angry – he could feel his temper rising – but he stopped himself. Then, suddenly, a laugh burst out from inside him as he realized that this battle with Devon could go on and on. This was Devon. Stubborn, clever Devon. If Jon loved him, he would have to accept him as he was.

"Hey, boy," he said to Homer, who was very relieved to see that Jon was happy again. "Come on down, Devon!" he shouted up the stairs. "It's OK." Devon rushed down the stairs when he realized he wasn't going to get into trouble, knocking Homer out of the way and leaping onto Jon's lap!

PROGRESS REPORT

ON DEVON AND HOMER

Homer and Devon are first cousins, but they couldn't be more different in lots of ways.

HOMER . . .

- Learns commands quickly. Within a week of his arrival he was housetrained, able to sit, heel, lie down (always the hardest) and walk off the lead. He does what I ask cheerfully
- Is obedient, bright and good-tempered
- Is happy being the underdog. He gives way to Devon and doesn't want to challenge him
- Has lots of doggy friends and loves people
- Loves Devon; he thinks of him like a bossy older brother

DEVON . . .

- *Still likes to test me. He is always waiting for a chance to be naughty*
- *Is mostly obedient nowadays. But he always needs to know why. I can't just bark a command and expect him to obey. He needs to know there's a point*
- *Insists on being top dog. He decides who chews what, gets fed first (sometimes he even grabs a chunk of Homer's food to show who's boss) and has first claim on me*
- *Doesn't naturally make friends with people _ though Homer is teaching him*
- *Loves Homer; he thinks of him like a sweet younger brother*

And both of them loved Jon! He often thought how lucky he was to have found two such wonderful dogs.

CHAPTER THIRTEEN

A Promise Kept

I promise you we'll go and find some real sheep as soon as things settle down, and you can herd them.

That was the promise Jon had made to Devon when the dog first submitted to him. It had been a roller-coaster ride since then, but now Jon felt that it was time to keep his promise. Devon was finally going to meet some sheep!

Jon and the dogs were heading for Raspberry Ridge Farm to meet Carolyn, who trained working dogs to herd. Jon thought she sounded perfect for

Devon and Homer: she praised her dogs when they obeyed and really seemed to adore animals. As they drove along, Devon and Homer looked out of the windows, their tongues hanging out expectantly. "Gentlemen," Jon told them solemnly, "this is the first day of the rest of your lives. You're going to meet your destiny!" Devon yelped with happiness. He and Homer could hear sheep baaing somewhere in the distance, and their ears pricked in anticipation!

Carolyn was a thin woman in her late thirties, dressed in an army camouflage jacket and carrying a shepherd's crook. After meeting the dogs she wasn't convinced that either of them would be able to herd at all – "We don't get many *Barbie* collies," she told Jon in her soft voice.

Jon didn't understand what she meant. "Barbie collies?" he asked, puzzled.

"That's what I call show dogs," Carolyn explained. "They usually don't have much herding instinct left; it's been bred out of them." She looked carefully at Jon, Devon and Homer for a moment before asking, "So why are you bringing your dogs all the way out here?"

This was a fair question. Jon knew that, to outsiders, Devon and Homer seemed to be doing just fine without sheep in their lives. But he had made Devon a promise, and he wanted to keep it. Poor Devon had herded buses, cars, people, squirrels and geese. Now Jon wanted him to have a chance to try it with sheep. And little Homer was growing up too: he was amazingly agile and would dive into ponds and catch mice on the run. Jon felt that he deserved a chance to use his skills and interact with some real livestock too.

Jon wondered how to explain all this to Carolyn. "It's a question of honour," he said finally. "I owe it to them. I love them and I want, if only for half an hour, to let them come face-to-face with what they have been bred to do for centuries. Just once, they ought to herd some sheep."

"A good answer," Carolyn said, smiling. "But still – Barbie collies . . ."

Jon grinned, it was now time to see what Devon

and Homer could do. Were they *Border* collies or *Barbie* collies? Their honour was at stake, but Jon was convinced they could prove Carolyn wrong.

An American Border collie, short-haired, lean, businesslike and grizzled – definitely a dog who had never seen shampoo – popped out of the barn to check out the new arrivals. He looked at Jon and then glanced at Devon and Homer and their well-groomed, flowing coats, before heading straight back towards the barn. To Jon, this dog's message was clear – *Barbie collies.*

"This is Dave," Carolyn said, gesturing to the handsome animal. "He's my assistant."

For the next fifteen minutes Jon and his dogs watched as Carolyn and Dave moved some sheep from the barn into a holding pen, then down a long path and into a field. Carolyn was patient and careful with the sheep, and she chose the best ones for Devon and Homer to work with – sheep who wouldn't be too frightened by inexperienced dogs.

The Border collies looked on jealously. Dave followed Carolyn's instructions carefully, keeping the sheep moving, circling them again and again. It was a perfect demonstration of what Devon and Homer should do.

"One dog at a time," Carolyn said, pointing to Homer first. "Oh, and watch the sheep, not your dogs," she told Jon. "If they come for you, turn sideways and usually they will part around you. If you feel them crashing into your legs, go down."

Jon was gobsmacked. He hadn't imagined that *he'd* be doing any herding. He had assumed that Carolyn would issue the instructions and he would just be watching proudly while Devon and Homer showed what they could do. And he'd never thought sheep could be *dangerous* – although they did look bigger and more bad-tempered than he had expected! He had no experience with livestock; no old instincts to draw on, and now he felt panicky.

"Oh, no," Carolyn explained with a smile as she saw the look on Jon's face. "This test isn't just for your dogs. Herding is something you do together."

Jon suddenly wanted to go home! He wasn't sure

he could do this. But when he looked at his dogs, he saw that they were watching Dave intently, their heads swivelling from side to side as if they were watching a fascinating tennis match. They were so tense with anticipation they looked like they might explode! Clearly, something inside them had switched on: herding was something they wanted to try – *now*! Jon knew he had to stick with it for them.

"Remember," Carolyn told him again just before he went into the field, "watch the *sheep*, not the dogs."

She ran through the herding commands for Jon and the dogs, demonstrating each one with Dave. Jon struggled to take them all in. The commands were:

"Fetch" – to drive the sheep to her.

"Gather" – for the dog to herd the sheep into a neat group.

"Go bye" – for the dog to circle to the left of the sheep.

"Way to me" – for the dog to circle to the right.

"Steady" — for the dog to slow to a creeping walk.

And "That'll do" (just like the farmer does in the movie *Babe*!) for the dog to know his work is over.

Jon was not sure *he* would remember all of them, let alone the dogs!

It was the moment of truth. He took a deep breath and tied Devon to a post before going into the field with Homer and shutting the gate behind them.

"Unleash him," Carolyn said calmly.

Homer's lead was barely off before he took off like a rocket from a launch pad, heading straight for Dave and the sheep. The woolly animals bleated nervously. Jon was tense too, but he needn't have worried. Homer behaved as if he had done this a hundred times before; as if it was totally natural to him. He ran round to the opposite side of the herd, joining Dave, and started to circle the sheep carefully.

Dave *had* done this hundreds of times. Calm and efficient, he moved the sheep simply by eyeing them, moving first in one direction, then in the other, looping back to collect strays, then retreating to a far corner to await Carolyn's next instruction.

As Homer ran behind the sheep, he no longer looked like the cute, cuddly dog who had crawled onto Paula's pillow that morning. Now he was a *fiend*.

He charged,

barked,

nipped,

and occasionally emerged from the herd with a mouthful of wool!

"Wow!" Carolyn was impressed. "He's a champ!" Homer, she told a very proud Jon, was using every trick in the book – his body, his teeth and his "eye" – to herd the sheep.

Jon was mesmerized by Homer's cleverness; how easily he moved! He watched, engrossed. Behind him he heard Devon barking furiously and pulling at his lead, but he paid no attention. Suddenly he knew why Devon had been barking: he was snapped out of his thoughts by Carolyn shouting, "Watch the sheep! Watch the sheep!" Five or six of them whirled round and headed for the gate, which Jon had foolishly stepped in front of. There was no time for him to get out of the way, so he quickly turned sideways. Thankfully the flock barged past him as the dog formerly known as Homer streaked past in a blur.

Homer was a natural! He passed the herding test with flying colours, even coming back to Jon's side as soon as he called him over. He looked exhausted, his tongue hanging out, but very, very happy and pleased with himself.

And then it was Devon's turn.

Nothing had ever come simply for Devon. And herding didn't now. He charged the sheep individually rather than herding them, going for chunks of wool rather than persuasion. The sheep were *not* happy. Nor was Devon. He looked very uncertain and nervous.

He lunged,

attacked,

ran over to Jon to rest his nose against his leg, raced from one end of the field to the other.

As he did so, he looked nervously at Jon and Carolyn: he knew this was something he *should* be able to do, but he just couldn't.

Jon felt so sorry for Devon; he wished he could get him out of there as he was clearly not as good at it as Homer. He was very surprised; Devon had seemed like a natural when he'd been herding buses!

Carolyn watched him closely; she had to admit that both Devon and Homer had surprised her and that they both had potential. Homer, she thought, was obviously a star, but she didn't want to write Devon off. She thought that Devon *needed* to herd. "He can't quite make sense of the world,' she said. "Herding could help to settle him down." She wanted to get more from Devon, and told Jon that she'd be happy to work with both dogs. They could and should herd.

Jon called the pair over when it was time to leave, and they padded up to him willingly.

"I'm impressed." Carolyn smiled. "It's obvious from how they obey you how much these guys trust you. You must have done a lot of work with them already. I'd love to take them for some herding classes."

Jon signed them up there and then!

CHAPTER FOURTEEN

Border Collie Heaven

At their next herding lesson, Carolyn first of all showed Jon how it should work and what he should do – the herder needed to be trained too. She used little plastic models of sheep, dogs and a herder to demonstrate to Jon how the herder should stand to one side of the sheep and the dog should go to the opposite side. And Jon needed to use a clicker to train the dogs.

When Homer went into the small field and saw the dozen sheep Carolyn had ready for him to practise on, he gave them the "eye". This was a good sign, and Jon expected Homer to be as impressive as he had been on their previous visit to Carolyn's farm. But today Homer was struggling. He paid very little attention to Jon and his clicker. He was far too interested in the sheep!

Jon was getting frustrated, but Carolyn reassured him. "It's no problem. He's young; he'll work it out."

The entire time Homer was in the field with the sheep, Devon watched him and Jon intently. And when it was his turn, he amazed both Carolyn and Jon. He made a wide circle around the pen – "squaring off", as it is called – until he was opposite the herder, exactly as he was supposed to.

Carolyn clicked, and Devon obeyed her.

Jon clapped and cheered in surprise.

Then Devon did it again.

Jon watched his Border collie proudly: he obviously hadn't enjoyed being second best to Homer at all! Was this clever, sleek dog the same dog who chased buses and leaped onto the roof of a passing van? he asked himself.

"Good guys, I'm proud of you," Jon told them both, scratching them behind their ears.

They beamed back at him.

Devon and Homer were happy with Jon and Paula in New York, but they both loved the freedom and space of the mountains. It was one of their favourite places in the whole world.

Some weeks after their first herding lesson, Jon took them up to his cabin on a special mission: he was going to scatter Julius and Stanley's ashes over the mountain they had loved so much. As soon as Jon started to load up the car, both dogs started circling him and yapping with excitement. They knew what was coming! When Jon went to fetch the old duffel bag he always took up there, Devon stuck his head inside, trying to climb into it – he couldn't wait to get there!

And four hours later, as they drove up the mountain road, Devon began to bark. Then Homer joined in, both dogs yapping noisily until they reached the cabin. As soon as Jon opened the car door, they shot out, raced into the woods and began chasing each other around the meadow. At times like this they were still the perpetual-motion machines they had always been. Insects didn't worry them. They didn't care what the weather was like. They just loved to run around.

Bobbing and weaving,

darting under and over and around logs and trees,

leaping into springs,

noticing every butterfly, mouse and wild turkey,

never stopping, continually circling, chasing – and enjoying every moment.

They were truly alive, down to the tips of their tails. And they were fantastic to watch!

Homer was bigger now, and more cunning than he had been when he was a tiny puppy. He knew exactly how to wind Devon up! He would vanish into the trees, or hide in the tall grass, reappearing every few minutes to bark, before disappearing again. His eyes gleamed with enjoyment. This was *fun*!

Devon tore after him but he couldn't always catch the faster, younger collie. When he finally did, he would grab him by the collar, throwing him to the ground. Homer played dead until Devon loosened his grip – then he shot off again! They played this game for hours, making Jon laugh out loud at their antics.

By the time it was getting dark, they were all exhausted. Jon lit a fire and they settled down in front of it, one dog on each side of his chair, until bedtime, all three of them lost in their thoughts.

Jon mused about his life with Devon and Homer – it was never simple, never as calm as his life had been before, with Julius and Stanley. But they had so much fun together that he now found it hard to remember how tricky those first few months with Devon had been, and how close he had come to admitting defeat.

When he eventually climbed into bed and turned off the light, Devon hopped quietly up onto the pillow on the other side of the bed, while Homer sneaked in at the foot. The dogs weren't supposed to spend the night on the bed, but they were all so content that, for now, Jon didn't care! The dogs were in Border collie heaven, and he was just as happy as they were!

It was midnight. There was a full moon and Jon woke suddenly, startled by the brightness of the light that was shining into the cabin bedroom. Homer was already awake, sitting up and staring through the window. When Jon got up, Devon was instantly alert, wanting to know what was up.

Jon pulled on his hiking boots and walked out onto the mountaintop. The moon was enormous – a big silver plate, bathing the valley in cool light and casting shadows along the fringes of the meadow – and he wanted a better look. The dogs padded out after him.

Devon and Homer loped across the stubbly grass of the open field to the pine trees below. They were not chasing each other, just galloping around in ever-widening circles, as free as the air.

Jon walked over to the spot where Julius had

always liked to sit and stare at the view. Earlier that day he had scattered Julius and Stanley's ashes there. A final farewell. The two dogs would now be reunited for ever. They still left big holes in Jon's heart, but the holes were slowly being filled by the need to think of the future; to think of Devon and Homer.

It had been almost twelve months since Devon had exploded into Jon's life at the airport, and now here he was on this mountain, watching two Border collies race about the meadow.

They had been a challenge in their different ways, but both had bought great happiness, and as Jon looked at them, he recognized how beautiful they were. Devon was sleekly jet-black and white now, and Homer had lost his puppy fur and was growing a new glossy, blue-tinged coat.

Jon clapped his hands to get their attention. "Time to go in, boys." It was cold out there.

They started to head towards him, but suddenly Devon froze before starting up again. His dark eyes were totally focused, and Jon saw him streaking in a straight line directly towards him. He wondered for a moment if Devon had spotted a deer or a fox behind him. And then he saw the look on Devon's face, and saw where he was aiming. Straight at Jon!

He threw his arms out wide and Devon leaped into the air, crashing into him, trusting that Jon would catch him. Jon could barely hold Devon's wriggling body as the dog lunged at his face, licking first one cheek and then the other, his bright eyes fierce with love.

This was a moment just for Devon and Jon. Homer was gambolling around in circles close by, but Jon knew exactly what this leap from Devon meant; what this collision on the mountaintop in the dead of the night showed. It had been a tough dog year, but the two of them had made it.

"We did it, boy!" Jon called in delight. *"We did it!"*

THE END

BORDER COLLIES

FACT FILE

- Border collies are a breed of herding dog that first appeared in the borders of England, Wales and Scotland. They were bred to work with sheep and other livestock but are also popular pets.

- Many of the best Border collies today can trace their lineage back to two dogs. Old Hemp was a champion in the late 1800s and won sheepdog trials all his life, never being beaten by another dog. He was tough on sheep and didn't like strangers. Old Kep was bred in the early 1900s, and he was much friendlier with people.

- They are very intelligent – possibly the most intelligent dogs in the world.

- They have loads and loads of energy and like lots and lots of exercise.

- They are happiest when they have a job to do. They like to work with a handler.

- The most common colour is black and white (like Devon).

- Working Border collies respond to the human voice or whistles at long distances. When working with sheep, a trained sheepdog can do the work of three people.

- Border collies can also make good search-and-rescue dogs in mountain and moorland areas.

- Border collies are very good at obedience and agility competitions as they are so fast and supple. One Border collie, Gin, appeared with his owner, Kate, on British television in the finals of Britain's Got Talent and amazed viewers with his dog dancing (a form of obedience).

- A Border collie named Striker holds the current Guinness World Record for opening a car window – in 11.34 seconds!

LABRADOR RETRIEVERS

FACT FILE

- Labrador retrievers are a type of gun dog, but they make excellent pets and are one of the most popular breeds of dog in the world.

- They were first bred on the island of Newfoundland in Canada and were used by fishermen to help with pulling nets in from the water – the dog swam out and grabbed the floating corks on the end of the nets and brought them in.

- They are quite big dogs. The average male will weigh 30–36 kg. They love eating so they sometimes eat too much and get a bit too fat.

- Their coats are usually either black, yellow or what is called chocolate (medium to dark brown).

• Their coats are water-repellent so they don't get cold if they go in the water in the winter. They also have webbed toes so they are great swimmers.

• They are gentle, clever, good-natured dogs and are particularly good with children.

• They have very soft mouths – a Labrador can carry an egg in its mouth without breaking it!

A WORD OF CAUTION

It's hard to meet – or read about – a Border collie and not want one for yourself. They are beautiful, intelligent dogs. But this breed isn't for everyone.

Nor are Labradors. Julius and Stanley were magnificent dogs, but they might not be the right breed of dog for you.

If you are thinking of getting a dog, do make sure you talk to breeders, vets and other owners and make sure that you get the right dog for you, and for your lifestyle. Border collies can be very difficult – there are lots of other breeds of dog to choose from.

Good rescue centres and dog breeders will always ask you lots of questions about your home and how much time you have available before they will let you have a dog. If they don't, you should go elsewhere.

You should always get a dog from a registered breeder, or from an official rescue centre. Never go to a pet shop as their puppies may have come from puppy farmers – breeders out to make a quick profit who may not care about the health and welfare of their puppies.

For further information on dogs and dog ownership in the UK:

The Kennel Club

The Kennel Club was founded in 1873 and aims to "promote in every way the general improvement of dogs". They can provide lots of information and advice on dog welfare, health, training and breeding. They can also put you in touch with registered breeders of different kinds of dog. The breeders on their register sign up to recommended breeding guidelines.

www.thekennelclub.org

The RSPCA

If you suspect a dog is being ill-treated or the owners

need some help in knowing what their dog needs – for example, a Border collie would find it almost intolerable being shut in a flat on its own all day – call the RSPCA, and they will be able to offer advice, or will call round to see the dog. They also offer lots of advice for dog owners, including advice on buying a puppy and finding the right breed for you.

www.rspca.org.uk

24-hour cruelty and advice line: 0300 1234 999

Border Collie Rescue

This registered charity takes in, cares for, rehabilitates, retrains and rehomes Border collies and working sheepdogs. They also provide lots of advice and information about the breed. They are based in the UK, but they have contact links to animal rescue groups in 127 different countries.

www.bordercollierescue.org

ACKNOWLEDGEMENTS

A Dog Year was first published as a longer book for adults, first in the USA and then in the UK. All the same thank-yous apply to this book too, including:

❖ My wife, Paula Span, who has shared my dog year.

❖ Deanne Veselka, owner and breeder of Border collies in Texas, who sent Devon and then Homer to me.

❖ Dr Brenda King, my vet, for helping me to face reality and deal with it compassionately.

❖ Ralph Fabbo, who first taught me to train dogs.

❖ Carolyn Wilki, for taking me to the next level.

❖ My daughter, Emma Span, for reminding me every day to keep laughing at myself, and at life.

Jon Katz

ABOUT THE AUTHOR

Jon Katz lives on Bedlam Farm in New York, USA, with his wife, Paula Span, and his dogs, sheep, donkeys, cat, irritable rooster Winston and three hens. He has written lots of books for adult readers and writes regular newspaper columns about dogs and about living in the country.

For further information,
see www.bedlamfarm.com.

Try these other fantastic titles from Random House Children's Books . . .

Christian the Lion
Based on the story of
Anthony Bourke and
John Rendall

The true story of one lion's search for a home . . .

For sale: lion cubs,
in Harrods department store!

Imagine the surprise on shoppers' faces
when they see a pair of beautiful little lion
cubs for sale in London! Two friends, Ace
and John, can't bear to leave the male cub
behind, stuck in such a tiny cage.

So they take him home with them, and
they name him Christian. But it's not long
before the cheeky lion is getting into all
sorts of mischief and sticky situations!

Whatever will they do when Christian
changes from a cute and cuddly little cub
into a powerful and noble beast . . .?

ISBN: 978 1 862 30956 2

THE CATLADY
By Dick King-Smith

Cats, cats . . . and more cats!

Muriel is known as the
Catlady because she lives
alone with just her many cats
for company. When a new kitten is born, it
soon becomes clear that it's no ordinary cat!
Vicky is a kitten with a very regal character,
and strangely enough, she was born on
the day that Queen Victoria died . . .

A purr-fect new tale from the bestselling,
award-winning, Dick King-Smith

ISBN: 978 0 552 55044 4